THE YOUNG VC'S HANDBOOK

A TACTICAL GUIDE FOR NEWCOMERS TO VENTURE CAPITAL

IN COLLABORATION WITH 50+ AUTHORS FROM THE INDUSTRY

Table of Contents

To stay up to date with the latest versions
of the book, scan below

Contributors

Ariel Purnsrian

Jadyn Bryden

Jesse Bloom

Michael Spiro

Yaz el Baba

James Hueston

Lili Rogowsky

Maya Menon

Nandini Agarwal

Paraj Mathur

Shomik Ghosh

Andrew Kallick

Kyle Perez

Pratyush Buddiga

Sakib Jamal

Will Shao

Charlie Liao

Chelsea Zhang

Gabi Marques

Jackson Bubala

Ryan Morgan

Dawit Heck

Enzo Wiener

Gabriella Garcia

J.P. Bowgen

Jeremy Navarro

Yuanling Yuan

Fred Kauber

Ian Goldberg

Kwesi Acquay

Taylor Davidson

Yoni Rechtman

Annia Mirza

Claire Pan

JC Bahr-de
Stefano

Taylor Brandt

Deek Velagandula

Desmond Fleming

Grant Miller

Joseph Lissak

Maliekah Harjani

Andrew Ciatto

Erik de Stefanis

Hammad Aslam

Jack Harvey

Juliette Rolnick

Aman Kandola

Andrew Rea

Jack McClelland

Matt Weinberg

Meghan Hillery

Molly Cline

Vaneezeh Siddiqui

William Leonard

Introduction & Acknowledgements

This book started with an attempt to solve a problem I faced myself – there are numerous guides that talk about getting into VC, but very few that compile tactical advice for junior roles. This is an attempt to bring together the best minds in venture capital and hear how they would answer some of the common queries new members of the industry may have.

How this Guide Works

You will notice each chapter is an attempt to present topics in digestible formats. Going by the same principle, this guide provides bite-sized exercises crowd-sourced from the best talent in VC today. The end-product is a 10-week course to cover the basics using real-world experience from our authors.

JAAGO partnership

I've had scholarships all my life. This book aims to give back – all proceeds from every purchase goes to the JAAGO foundation, with the funds allocated towards building a new primary school in Bangladesh, a country of 170+ million people in South Asia. Since 2007, JAAGO has been operating schools for thousands of underprivileged children all over the country. Thousands of disadvantaged children receive quality education free of cost through their work. In 2017, JAAGO was recognized by UNESCO for their outstanding work. You can learn more at jaago.com.bd

This is a crowd-sourced book, and credit belongs to each section's author – all of whom I'm immensely grateful to for supporting this project, and children's education in Bangladesh through JAAGO as a result.

—

I would like to thank my maa, baba and apee for making immense sacrifices for my own education throughout life. I would also like to thank my friends Kinza and Fateen for helping me with ideation and edits. In addition, I owe gratitude to friends who became family at my toughest times - Mahrusah Zahin, Eva Jahan, Donna Sitwat, Faria Kamal, Maheeb Chowdhury, and to my partner, Juma for all your support and patience. My teachers in Myanmar, Sunbeams Dhaka and United World College of Hong Kong, along with everyone who helped me through my formative years at Cornell and JP Morgan.

Lastly, a big shoutout to my mentors who took a chance on me and taught me the art of venture capital - Ali Hamed, Savneet Singh, Ryan Morgan and many others throughout the journey. It takes a village indeed.

Disclaimer

While we wrote this book utilizing our experience at our respective firms, the opinions expressed within are those of the listed authors. Any examples presented in this book are for illustrative purposes only and do not represent the performance of any investments.

Foreword

Howard Lindzon

I love to invest. It is a privilege to do so for a living.

I became an internet angel/seed investor at the end of 1999 as the internet bubble was about to burst. At the time, I was a hedge fund investor/manager, but like most young investors have recently witnessed in 2021 and 2022, I got caught up in the FOMO (fear of missing out) of Web 1.0 and invested in a late stage private company called CarsDirect.com. Along with that investment I received shares in another internet company startup called Viva.com. Long story short, Viva pivoted and survived as Rent.com, was acquired for $450 million by Ebay and I had made my first great (yes lucky) seed stage internet investment. A decade later CarsDirect.com would sell for pennies on the dollar but I was ahead and ready for the next wave which started again in 2005 with the birth of Web 2.0.

I learned that luck matters but more importantly, the founders of Viva/Rent.com were special and backing great founders and teams was key. They had incredible business sense, excellent fundraising skills and deep real estate domain experience. I was smart enough to always offer help to Scott Ingraham a co-founder and CEO of the company and not only have we remained friends but he has been a long time LP in our Social Leverage funds and together back in 2006 he was an investor and board member with me in GolfNow.com which we helped build and scale. GolfNow was eventually acquired by ComcastComcast (they own the Golf Channel).

The Web 2.0 boom that kicked off in 2006 was incredible. Growth seemed never ending and we had zero percent interest rates for almost a decade (ZIRP). Mobile and global domination was the goal for every startup.

As the cloud, the iPhone and social networks proliferated, the internet onboarded billions of newly networked people between 2009 and today. Hundreds of millions were new investors trading on Robinhood and Coinbase in North America alone. Thousands of young investors were setting up their first fund/rolling fund on Angellist and participating as LP's in their friends' funds. By 2021, everyone wanted to be a 'venture capitalist'. Much like the 80's and 90's where everyone wanted to be an investment banker, this did not end well. These new investors have now experienced their first bear market in stocks and private markets.

Flash forward to the summer of 2023 and the US venture capital market is in rapid decline:

"Only 6.1% of active startups on AngelList raised a round or exited in 1Q23, the lowest rate ever observed in our dataset. This rate of investment activity is a 1.3% decline from 4Q22's rate of 7.4%, and a 5% decline from 1Q22's rate of 11.6%."[1]

---

[1] To learn more, visit: https://www.angellist.com/assets/AngelList_State_of_Venture_1Q23.pdf

For those that do not remember the end of the bubble in March 2000, this chart may help:

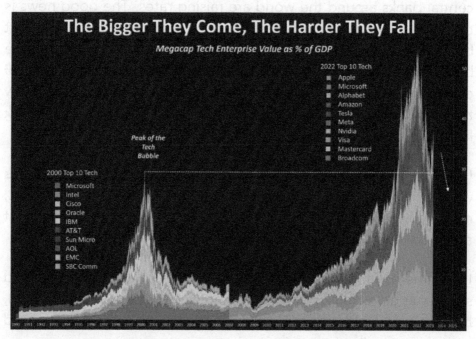

Source: Bloomberg, Kevin Smith - taken from Crescat Capital

Welcome to the world of investing.

So what does the future of venture capital look like and What advice do I have for newcomers?

The only answer is 'nobody knows'. I don't know myself. Guessing where the markets will be is a giant time suck and fools game. But, I was asked to lay out some ideas for the purpose of this book and so I will do so.

As interest rates rise, valuations compress. It is harder to raise and borrow money while capital is constrained. Countries look inward and markets shrink. Welcome to the textbook boring answer.

Another very high level textbook indicator is the old line *'do not fight the fed'*. Right now (August 2023) the US federal reserve and central banks around the world are raising rates. The good news is that markets move in cycles, and money never sleeps, so the next bull market is taking shape as you read this. I have no idea what the best start-up companies will be, and from what industries they will come, and what the founders' backgrounds will look like. I do know that as the last cycle ends, the next bull market does not usually look like the previous one.

I imagine that continued areas of rapid innovation and investments will continue with space, logistics, climate, alternative energy, robots, medicine, healthcare, Web3, AI, education, wealth management and e-commerce.

I think there is always room for generalists and specialists. I have had success as an incrementalist (not trying to invent the next big thing), but the world of Venture Capital needs longer term thinking and investing as well.

Being curious has served me well as a venture capitalist/angel investor.

1. I like to say great investors use their eyes, ears, hands and feet.

2. Being good with the keyboard - in my case blogging daily for 17 years - has also been a huge long-term boost to my network and career.

3. Hopping on a plane to meet face to face is underrated. My job as an investor is to talk to as many smart founders and investors as I can.

I believe the next wave of great venture capital returns will come from smaller funds. I have invested in some great small funds myself over the years including David Cohen's Bullet Time Ventures and Multicoin Capital. Both funds were under $10 million and have so far returned over 20 times my capital. I am likely biased by my experience, but the best investors I know, were investors that kept their fund sizes small (under $150 million).

I can't quantify it, but I know that being a public market investor helped me be a better private market investor. In 2023, every investor over 18 years old can and should have a Robinhood and Coinbase account to learn how markets work and more importantly how you work when real money is on the line.

It is also very important to find great mentors and the right investors to model behavior. That may come from asking or just eavesdropping and being gracious and nice on social media. Thank-you's add up.

Build domain experience, preferably around your passions. In a world both shrunk and expanded by technology, the niches contain great riches.

Get used to telling smart, passionate people NO. Sometimes sitting on your hands for years is the best investing you can do.

You will get so much advice as you embark on a career investing, so never forget you can also keep it simple. I love a Jason Zweig blog post titled *'The Seven Virtues of Great Investors'*.[2]

Curiosity, Skepticism, Independence, Humility, Discipline, Patience, Courage.

Best of luck.

---

[2] https://jasonzweig.com/the-seven-virtues-of-great-investors/

WEEK 1

BUILDING INFRASTRUCTURE & A NETWORK

Day 1: **How do you stay organized as a VC?**

Michael Spiro – Insight Partners

Staying organized is one of the most important aspects of any job, particularly in venture, where you may have X potential investments in the pipeline, Y projects to help portfolio companies with, and Z exciting companies / founders you want to meet.

Prioritizing organization is critical to success in venture.

My advice: spend time on organization now, so that you save a lot more time later.

Figuring out your "organization stack" likely won't come in one try. It may even change over time. But, paying close attention to how you organize your days, workflows, etc. is critical to freeing up time and enabling you to be as successful in your role as possible.

The day-to-day can get busy as a VC. As such, I think it's helpful to have a set structure with respect to how you schedule your days.

How I go typically about this:

8:30-10am: No calls. I find that I am not as productive before 10am. I do my best to not schedule calls early in the morning. Instead, I use this time to source companies, read the news / learn about recent funding rounds, and schedule calls / meetings for the coming weeks.

10am-12pm: Calls / meetings

12-1pm: Lunch & emails

1-3:30pm: Calls / meetings

3:30-6pm: Diligence, sourcing, and putting out the "fires" that may have popped up during the day

6-7:30pm: Workout & dinner

8-sleep: Emails and reading

While I find myself sometimes straying away from this structure, having this as a backbone is incredibly helpful in helping me stay organized. I do my best to finish every day at Inbox Zero, as it makes me feel I have 'completed' all of my to-do items. No Superhuman, no other add-ons, just Outlook and determination.

Exercise

I prioritize working out every day, as it keeps me sharp and up-to-speed. I prefer to work out in the early evening, as it gives me an energy boost to get a few more hours of work done after dinner. As the day gets busier, it gets difficult to find time to exercise, but it's a must-do for me. I find it to be immensely helpful in allowing me to reset and get my blood flowing. I always recommend doing some type of movement, even if it's a walk during a call, as it separates you from your desk and allows a clearer perspective.

Keeping Track of Deal Flow

As interesting companies & live deals pop up, it can become challenging to manage everything on your plate, in the pipeline, etc. One of the best pieces of advice I got early in my venture life was to create a system for managing deal flow.

Everyone's system here will be different. There is no one-size-fits-all model. You need something that works for you. A rough outline of my model is below:

Deal Flow					
Stay Close 1	Actively Raising 1	Due Diligence 1	TS 1	Won! 1	Passed / Lost 0
Company A	Company C	Company D	Company E	Company F	+ New
Company B	+ New	+ New	+ New	+ New	
+ New					

It's simple, but it gets the job done. While I think most of the areas are self-explainable, I'll dive into how I classify each category:

1. Stay Close

1. These are companies that I want to stay close to, but that aren't actionable for us yet, typically because of one of two reasons: it is too early and / or they are not currently fundraising.

2. I try to check-in with these businesses over email / phone every few months to see how things are going, see how I can help, and see if a fundraise may be more actionable.

1. Actively Raising

1. These are companies that are actively raising (or will be soon), where we have not yet stepped on the gas with respect to due diligence.

2. I group companies in this column into two buckets: (1) additional teammates already looped in; (2) additional teammates to be looped in

2. Due Diligence

1. These are companies we are actively diligencing. These are typically companies that are formally fundraising, though this also includes companies that are not currently raising, but where I want to get to know the business / space well in advance of a future raise.

2. Every firm / individual goes about diligence quite differently. Diligence, in itself, can get hectic, so I recommend also setting in place a template / guide to help you stay on top of everything related to diligence that you are doing. I have not yet fully optimized my organization here - if you find something that works for you, let me know!

3. TS

These are companies where we have issued a Term Sheet.

4. Won!

These are rounds we won (and invested in)! I add companies to this bucket once the round is formally closed and the money is wired.

The goal here, as you have probably caught on to, is to move a company from left to right. The more companies on the right, the better. If we pass on a company (or lose the round), I add those companies to a separate board. I check-in with these companies every few months, too, to see if we may be a good fit for a future round.

That's all from me. I hope this adds some light as you think about how to best stay organized while working in venture. If you have any questions, comments, or feedback, let me know. My email is mspiro [at] insightpartners [dot] com, and I am on Twitter @mspiro3.

Day 2: **How should VCs prioritize their time?**

Yaz El-Baba – Emergence Capital

Any person early in their career learns that one of the most difficult exercises to manage is the art of prioritization. Especially as you get started in venture, you realize that there is no standard model for how to succeed in this business. Over time, the number of responsibilities you juggle can become unbearingly overwhelming. The purpose of this guide is to help individuals early in their venture career understand how I view the core buckets of work, and how to best prioritize across them.

1. Sourcing

Junior investors are expected to source great opportunities for the firm. Your value increases as you become "in the flow" of information and can surface these opportunities to the firm at the right time. This can be a daunting expectation early on in your venture career, since most junior people do not have a long career of relationships to lean on for deal information.

My suggestion? As opposed to brute-forcing inorganic, relationship-driven sourcing efforts – focus on where you can provide immediate value: data-driven and research-driven deal sourcing. As you build a repertoire of insights and companies to speak about, you'll then be far better equipped to build stronger relationships, which will in turn increase the quality (and quantity) of your relationship-driven leads.

2. Sourcing Operations

Think of Sourcing Ops as the venture analog to Sales Ops. As a junior VC, one of your superpowers is the visibility into all of the internal context within a firm. You are best suited to know what lead is most appropriate for what partner (at the right time). By focusing your energy here, you both help your firm avoid deal slippage, and help CEOs navigate internal firm dynamics towards the highest likelihood of success.

My suggestion? While this isn't the sexiest place to spend your time, over-index here early as you build trust within your partnership, and with CEOs.

3. Deal Work

A live deal can (and will) blow up your perfectly prioritized work schedule. Be prepared for these hyper intense periods. Two suggestions with how to deal with live deals:

1. Deals take precedence over everything else. Meetings get rescheduled often. If you are chasing after a live deal, respectfully push out your coffee chats, and other lower-priority meetings.

2. Get in the habit of "getting smart" on a company before a company is actively fundraising. That way, you can frontload a lot of the time-consuming market and competitive work ahead of a quick process.

4. Portfolio Work

Every firm is different here. In my experience, portfolio work ramps as you get to know more of your portcos at the time of investment (since they'll know you more personally, they'll feel more comfortable reaching out to you for help). There are many ways to help your portcos. A few suggestions:

1. As a junior VC, you are well-positioned to help entrepreneurs with their fundraising. Prioritize the energy early on to build your own rolodex of pitch deck / data room templates, follow-on investor lists, and best practices. You will undoubtedly be asked to help portcos with fundraising - by frontloading the hard work early, you've baked in a ton of high-value leverage.

2. Beyond fundraising, choose 1 or 2 areas that you want to be known as a subject matter expert in (e.g., hiring customer success talent, building financial forecasts, sales plans, etc.), where you can become a strategic value add.

3. Choose a few companies to go deep with. While your urge may be to help every company in the portfolio, know that your time here is limited. Spend as much time as you can with the companies where you have a direct relationship with the team, and where they need the most help.

5. Brand Building

I view brand building as two distinct sub-segments: internal and external. You build a brand for yourself internally by the types of projects and work you become known for being exceptional at. Your brand internally will help you build trust amongst your team!

External brand building takes on many different flavors: Twitter, deep content, events, etc. Figure out what style is most authentic to you, and budget regularly cadenced time to devote against it.

These are, in my opinion, the core buckets of a successful venture career. There may be other miscellaneous items that do not fit perfectly into this non-exhaustive list. However, these capture the most common activities you must juggle early in a venture career. Understanding what to prioritize vs. others is hyper-dependent on you and your firm, though, knowing how to contextualize where your time is being spent among these buckets is the first step in understanding how you should be spending your time moving forward!

Day 3: **What are the basics of "networking"?**

Jadyn Bryden – Xfund

Why is networking so important?

Networking is the way to grow your personal and professional community as an adult. You may have heard the age-old saying, "It's not what you know, it's who you know," and this alludes to the importance of networking. In the world of venture capital, relationships are the name of the game. So how do you do it? Let's break down some ways to make networking seem less daunting and rather approachable– or dare I say fun!

1. Framework

It is important to approach networking in a non-transactional posture. Think of networking as a process by which you are building friendships and learning about the lives of other people. Ponder what you can do for others. Ask yourself what connections and introductions you can make for the person you're meeting. Of course, you'll also want to think about what ways you need help, but this won't be the main focus or obvious agenda when networking. Begin new relationships with the mindset: how can I add value?

2. Walking into the Room

Walking into a room by yourself with a bunch of people you don't know can be extremely daunting. Amidst all the people chatting, many networking events have food and drink of some sort. An easy way to enter the room and warm yourself up for a night of networking is to start off by surveying the room as you walk over to grab yourself a drink. If there is alcohol, take it easy – you might even consider not drinking at all – because you want to be in good shape to make the best first impressions. After you have your club soda and lime, it's go-time. If you see anyone standing off by themselves, go say hi and introduce yourself. That person is sure to feel relieved to have someone to talk to and you'll be able to start off your night with a simple one-on-one conversation. If there are no singletons in the mix, find a group of people who look approachable and walk up to the group. Do not be afraid to interrupt because people come to networking events expecting to mingle and meet new people. You can approach the circle of people and politely ask if you can join the conversation. Typically people will welcome you in so you can introduce yourself briefly and ask them to resume the conversation. Find points of connection with people's stories that you relate to and feel free to have side conversations with the people standing immediately to your right and left. Once the ball is rolling, your initial nerves from being in a new room with a bunch of new people should wear off.

3. Conversation Starters

If you're wondering how to start the conversation, here are a few quick ones to keep in mind:

- So, what do you do for work?

- How long have you lived in (fill in the blank with the city you're in)?

- What keeps you busy these days?

- What brought you out to the event?

- How do you like working in (venture capital/entrepreneurship/ fill in the blank)?

- What's your take on (fill in the blank with non-controversial tech news)?

4. Graceful Exit

You've had a great conversation with your new connection but now it's time to move on and meet some new people. Or perhaps, the conversation is generally not as exciting as you expected and it's time for a change. Here are a few ways to politely make your exit:

- Well so great to meet you, I'm going to continue making rounds and meeting some other new people, let's stay in touch.

- Who else do you think I should meet? Would you mind introducing me?

- I'm going to refresh my glass.

- I'm going to go check out the cheese selection, great meeting you!

5. Follow Up

A good networking event is not complete without personalized follow-ups. After the event, it is important to make a connection online with the people you met in person. It is easy to forget names and faces when you meet many people at one event. Follow-up can be as simple as adding your new acquaintances on Linked In or as in-depth as sending an email or text the next day. Good networking practice is to maintain a personal "CRM" (customer relationship management) tool to take notes and remember important information about the people you meet at networking events. Notes might include the type of investments a VC makes, what area a founder is building in, and other similar types of details.

Pro Tips

- Don't feel like you need to meet everyone in the room. Focus on a few high-quality interactions. I have a one-person rule. I try to leave every event having met one person who I will follow up with to ensure that I at least have one great reason I went to an event.

- Be authentic.

- Don't let your eyes wander around the room while you are talking to someone. Be present in every interaction.

- Don't hand out your business card unless someone asks for it. Also, look into a digital business card. These cards save the earth and make sharing your contact info as easy as one tap.

- Learn how to use the LinkedIn scan feature – just trust me.

- Set a timer with an audible alarm if you want to have an exit strategy for when you need to leave.

Conclusion

Networking is the fun part of the job of a venture capitalist. Many evenings will be spent at events meeting other investors and amazing founders. Finding ways to maximize your time and impact at these events while still having fun is a skill worth refining. When these strategies are implemented, networking events can be the activity that recharges you, rather than an energy drain. Remember to have fun with it! Go forth and network!

Day 4: **What drives your personal brand?**

Ariel Purnsrian – Venture Investor, Formerly at Fifth Wall

You're a new venture capitalist and it's your first day on the job. Congratulations, you've worked hard to land this competitive role and the time has finally come! You've memorized Secrets of Sand Hill Road and you've read every TechCrunch article over the last 6 months. You feel that there is still so much you don't know — reluctance, excitement, ambition, doubt, yearning — all consume you. But you read between the lines, and remind yourself that you are ready to embark on this exciting journey.

As you ramp up, here is a short playbook on how to set yourself up for a successful career in VC. As a young female VC, I've drawn upon my learnings, triumphs, and pitfalls to provide you with a raw guide on how to navigate your first year. Remember, the opportunity is yours, you just can't be afraid to seize it.

Time is your most valuable asset, so use it wisely – your track record eventually becomes your brand

In an industry where speed of conviction makes all the difference, it is essential to have a targeted and methodical approach to evaluating investment opportunities. At one point or another you will find yourself feeling overwhelmed with the number of opportunities thrown at you all at once. To ensure you're able to evaluate investments efficiently and accurately:

1. aim to get in as many reps as early as possible.

2. Implement a "quick and dirty" filtering process to determine which opportunities deserve deeper diligence. Develop a thesis-driven framework for evaluating investments.

1. Experience: To acquire the skills and confidence needed to succeed in this role, aim to get in as many reps as early as possible. In my first year on the job, I took hundreds of founder calls, knowing many were not immediately actionable or directly in-scope of my mandate. Why? With each rep, I gained valuable experience which helped me sharpen my investing instincts and diligence opportunities with greater speed and conviction.

2. Quick & Dirty Diligence: Not all investment opportunities are created equal. Doing preliminary diligence up-front will enable you to filter out bad investments quickly while allowing you to spend more energy on the ones deserving of your time. As a general matter, I try to analyze growth rates, margins, capital efficiency, unit economics, TAM, competitive differentiation, PMF and strength of team ASAP in order to determine whether an opportunity is worth taking to the next level[1]. However, it is important to remember that "strong" metrics are relative to industry, geography and business model, so be sure to think about these measures within the right context.

3. Thesis-Driven Investing Framework: Great investors create thesis-driven frameworks from which they can reliably and quickly evaluate investments. For each applicable investment vertical, you should conduct market research and analysis to develop a 5-10 year view on the industry's trajectory. With this long-term view in mind, you should establish clear and comparable goalposts for determining what a good investment opportunity looks like that aligns with your

---

[1] See section in Week 4, Day 4 for more on the topic

thesis. Because you will always be comparing potential investments using the same objective criteria, your framework will enable you to evaluate opportunities with greater speed and accuracy.

Being a confident executor, presenter and most importantly, seller can build your reputation internally in the firm and externally to other investors and founders

Effective communication is important for any job, but is particularly important for a venture capitalist. Early on, you will find yourself speaking to founders, investment committees and even other VCs on a regular basis. It may sound elementary, but there are a few key communication points worth highlighting:

First, *how* you say something can be just as important as *what* you are saying. Regardless of your audience, remember to speak with conviction and be thoughtful about your responses. Remember also to ask meaningful questions of your own (those that are not easily Googleable, of course).

Another key but underappreciated communication skill is active listening. Especially in the context of presenting to an investment committee, make sure that you listen closely to the questions and concerns of those you are speaking with. Answer them directly. Oftentimes, people get so consumed with what they are going to say that they (unintentionally) disregard the point their counterparty is making. This is avoidable!

Most importantly, a great venture capitalist is also a great salesperson. What will you be selling? You'll be selling both yourself and your firm. This is especially true when speaking to founders. You will need to be prepared to answer why a founder should take your money instead of someone else's. Here, internalizing your firm's strategic value-add and also communicating your own personal strengths will be the key to winning competitive allocations.

Building a brand and expanding your network is the most powerful thing you didn't know you needed

Personal branding is essential to building a strong reputation and attracting deal flow. Many firms invest in marketing to 1) attract high quality deal opportunities 2) provide a valuable marketing platform to their portfolio companies and 3) educate society on their investment thesis.

The venture community is small and your network will be a great source of deal flow if you've taken the time to develop deep and meaningful relationships. Attend conferences, reach out to grab coffee, share deals and go the extra mile for others. Remember, you never know where your next deal or opportunity will come from.

Social media can also be a great tool for expanding your network. If you haven't downloaded Twitter, that would be a great place to start. Afterwards, start browsing through other social media sites (LinkedIn for professional posts, Medium for blogging, TikTok and YouTube for video creation), and take note of how influential investors are leveraging these platforms to brand themselves and make new connections.

Finally, remember to always act with integrity because your reputation carries a lot of weight. How you do anything, is how you do everything – so be consistent in your work ethic, your character and your ambition to level up - I can't wait for your success!

Day 5: **How should VCs utilize a CRM?**

Jesse Bloom – SaaS Ventures

A diverse network is a junior VC's most valuable asset, but a network can only be nurtured and deployed properly if it's well-organized using a customer relationship management tool (CRM). Without a flexible, integrated, and up-to-date CRM, a junior VC will fail to efficiently source deals, conduct diligence, support portfolio companies, and track activity. Here are my top 10 tips for junior VCs to master the CRM.

1. Commit to becoming the CRM champion in your fund

Spend extra time learning all the features, bugs, and use cases of your fund's CRM system. Get to know the support staff, administrative settings, and available integrations. As a junior VC, you will dramatically increase your value to the fund if you become its foremost expert on its most critical software.

2. Reduce as much friction to data capture as possible

Partners and staff at VC funds are busy, reduce as much friction as possible to capturing actionable data within the system. Automate as much as possible and reduce unnecessary intermediate actions. For example, take meeting notes directly in your CRM instead of hand-writing notes and then copying into the CRM later.

3. Maximize 'searchable' data

Data that is stored in a format that can be filtered or searched for within the full database is searchable data, compared to 'dead' data which can only be found by happenstance or through a tedious investigation. If John invests in early-stage fintech, then you should store that data in a field through which you can quickly filter for all the investors that invest in early-stage fintech. Searchable data is actionable, improvable, and presentable; strive to make all data searchable.

4. Supplement your data with publicly available information

If you can integrate your CRM with Pitchbook, Crunchbase, or any other useful database, you will save loads of time screen switching, and your data will be supercharged with non-obvious insights. Additionally, integrations with data cleansers like Apollo.io or Live Data Technologies will help you avoid the hassle that comes with email bounces.

5. Integrate your CRM into your workflow

Utilize your CRM in as many of your daily tasks as possible, otherwise you will lose valuable opportunities to log live data. CRMs are often flexible enough to accommodate idiosyncratic processes. Update and customize your CRM to make yours and your team's life easier.

6. Use your CRM to track activity, ideally activity directly tied to compensation

Use your CRM to "over-communicate" your level of activity over time, especially activity that is directly connected to compensation, such as sourcing activity (calls/meetings) and deals (sourced/diligenced).

Partners are too busy to track your every move, but when it's time for your review, you will be happy you tracked every encounter in a way that can be easily presented.

7. Utilize software connectors where your CRM lacks functionality

Software connectors such as Zapier and Tray.io can improve a junior VC's life dramatically by automating repetitive tasks within your daily workflow and keeping data accurate. Partners will be impressed by your initiative and productivity. For example, use Zapier to automatically post a Slack update whenever there is a portfolio company update in the CRM.

8. Integrate processes that naturally audit CRM data

Contact data will change rapidly as people switch jobs. CRM data accuracy is only as good as the team's data auditing process. Integrate a process into your workflow that forces team members to update stale information. For example, organizing your newsletter distribution list through your CRM, instead of a third party solution, will force team actions that will keep CRM data cleaner.

9. Have clear CRM policies and utilize templates

Work with your team to understand or develop policies related to data capture that directly support initiatives that are stated priorities for the partnership. A CRM will be much less effective if each team member is using it differently. Don't be afraid to make certain fields mandatory if they are critical and utilize note templates for each type of meeting to gently remind teammates what data is expected to be gathered.

10.Use your CRM to become a 'super-connector'

A well-organized CRM can be invaluable to a junior VC and his/her network. Stock your CRM with the information most useful to your team and your network, then volunteer your CRM as a resource for others to help with recruiting, diligence, deal sourcing, and any other ways it can be helpful. Experiment with gathering different types of information to test its value and utilize information to plan events or make valuable introductions before data goes stale. The more you offer your CRM to the community, the more you will become known for helping people, and the greater your personal brand will become.

WEEK 2

FINDING OPPORTUNITIES OR "SOURCING"

Day 1: **How do you build relationships past networking?**

Nandini Agarwal – ffVC

Quick Answer: VCs are known to be transactional and cliquey- Be better. I know it's easier said than done. While most people are chasing hot deals and sharpening their elbows, they tend to forget that being an investor is inherently a lonely job. Here's a quick guide to avoid the social pitfalls while you climb the ladder of success as an investor.

Earlier today I was interviewing candidates for an associate position at my current company, ffVC. When I inquired about what they qualify as their superpower, over half the candidates said something along the lines of managing and growing interpersonal relationships. Emotional intelligence is one of the strongest skills that a VC investor needs to have. But cultivating relationships in a competitive industry can be tough for someone who has high EQ, high IQ and is ambitious. None of us know if we are "good investors" until years later, and even then, the evaluation of the entry point might show that the reality of the fate of a company couldn't have been predicted, due to product pivots or team changes. Success metrics in this industry for a junior investor, can be very murky. So, my fellow high-achieving buds, you might ask, how do we measure success?

VC is a long game and one where we need to have a lot of shots on goal. Everyone wants to find the next unicorn, but there are two determinants to doing so: access and identification. If one can't recognize and act quickly on a golden opportunity, access can be meaningless, and vice versa. While mentorship from a seasoned VC is important, a junior investor can also lean on his/her peers and learn from one another.

Each VC relationship boils down to being resourceful, timely, dependable, and trustworthy. I have spent a considerable amount of time, cultivating genuine relationships with other investors who may become fund managers, entrepreneurs, or just great beachside bed & bar co-owners (at least that's my post-retirement plan) in the future. And it was through these relationships that I helped close more than twenty-five million dollars in follow-on funding for my portcos and sourced and led two investments, in the span of a year.

Here's my secret sauce for:

Inter-VC Relationships

1. Be respectful to gatekeepers

There's a lot of conversation within founder circles, around junior investors and whether they unintentionally gatekeep moonshot investments from more senior team members, but if we, as junior investors don't respect our friends' titles and their fund's hierarchical dynamics, how are we supposed to command the respect of founders? While an analyst or intern or CoS may not be your desired Point of Contact in another fund, treating them with the same respect and camaraderie will take you a long way. Even if you're connected with an individual on the platform or operations team, nurturing that relationship with the same essence will harbor great returns in the long run. They may not have decision-making power from an investment perspective but have the ear and attention of those who do. And actions of disrespect speak the loudest.

For example: Don't try to climb the food chain and ignore your friend who has a junior title, if you meet their manager. Respect your internal contact because they can be your biggest advocate or the lack thereof.

2. Earn your asks

Before you can ask for allocation in highly sought-after live deals, you need to create a reputation as someone who knows what one looks like. Every month, take the time to send out some high-quality vetted deals to other investors. These might be portfolio companies who are raising follow-on funding or deals that are not a fit for your fund due to stage/traction/sector or simply because you don't have internal buy-in from IC to lead the deal. Being top of mind is half the battle. And eventually the flywheel of deals will be set in motion by other investors. Just have your fund's pitch ready and a couple of niche areas of sector-based interests that set you apart from others.

Founders that you go out of your way to help out with fundraising will also, hold you in high regard and be willing to refer their friends who are building startups, to you. Being a super-connector can accelerate the "top of mind effect" as you will come up in other people's conversations and you will be remembered as the source of the connection. Making introductions within the investor network can also help you build a reputation as someone who believes in collaboration and takes a genuine interest in connecting like-minded folks.

Maintain a database to keep track of what other investors invest in and set up bimonthly/quarterly catchups to chat and share deal flow. A time-efficient way is to maintain a database of horizontally aligned investors. Create 3 buckets of investors: 1) investors who are a stage or two before yours, 2) a similar stage/sector as yours 3) a stage or two after yours, and over time you can push a relevant list of startups, every quarter using 3 separate bcc'd email chains.

– This is how I maintain my Database:

Fund Name

City

State

Country

Contact (First and Last Name)

LinkedIn URL

Contact Email

Contact Phone Number

Fund Website

Latest Fund Size

Verticals

Stage

Target Check Size/Ownership

Average Check Size (Min)

Average Check Size (Max)

Target Revenue (Minimum ARR)

Geographical/DEI Focus

Lead, Co-Lead, Follow on strategy

Deals Sent to me

Deals sent by me

1. Show up and lend support

Junior VCs hail from a variety of backgrounds. Some of us have a strong quantitative background and can model waterfalls and cap table models in our sleep and some of us are technical and can understand product builds with great detail. Everyone has a unique skill set and knowing your superpower can allow you to flourish. It's a lifelong journey of constant learning and iteration to be a great investor and supporting each other through this journey can be very impactful. If you think you have nothing specific to offer to a fellow VC, offer up your time. Show up to the happy hours and dinners they are hosting, help them connect them to your college friend who is working in the industry they're diligencing or simply buy them a drink after their struggle with an IC Memo deadline. The shoulder that you lend will possibly mean more to them than anything else.

2. Find your tribe

In big ecosystems like NYC and SF, where there are hundreds, if not thousands of VC investors, it can be a bit disillusioning and overwhelming to parse through the community. It's an arduous task to find people that you can rely on and share deeper conversations with, than those revolving around deals and decks. This job truly blends the lines between personal and professional lives so identifying those people on whom you can lean for both advice and a good time, is key. You don't need to necessarily rush or force connections because you will slowly identify other junior investors that you respect, perhaps because of their perspective on different verticals, or how they treat founders or their conduct even after a few drinks at a happy hour. You will slowly gravitate towards the individuals that you would like to associate yourself with both on a personal and professional level and find your "cohort". Just trust your gut instinct and give everyone a fair chance to be part of your inner circle.

3. Source with intent

Unless you have KPIs set by your firm on the number of companies to be sourced every week, it can be daunting to source deals that are of good quality and quantity. As people who are paid to be curious, it can be mentally and physically exhausting knowing that we are always on the job and on the move.

Trust me you're not alone. I talk to my Uber drivers to learn more about the inefficiencies in their other jobs & and industries: I have gathered insights on the issues in exporting fresh flowers internationally, and a lack of marketing solutions for home chefs and bakers in suburbs, among my conversations. I keep a small notebook with me, writing down ideas and frustrations I overhear from people on trains, planes, and at cafes: wealth-tech solutions needed specifically for managing estates of blended marriages, a consumer-facing wallet app to simplify and manage 401K rollovers, Zapier for setting up frictionless e-commerce stores on Amazon.

And while thinking through these gaps in the market is a good mental exercise, finding that a startup solution already exists, is rewarding, and a good source of deal flow. I also spend a lot of time sourcing from CVCs who can give me a quick gut check as both a financial investor and a potential customer. I also tend to source from geographies that aren't seen as the main hubs of innovation but have growing ecosystems of second-time founders who move closer to their families/hometowns after the hustle and bustle of NYC/SF, after getting a big payday from their first startup: the Midwest and the Southeast. You can't be everywhere, all the time so make friends that are boots on the ground, across geographies and sectors, and you'll be sure to find deals that are high quality for your fund.

VC- Founder relationships:

1. Pay attention

It's very easy to jump on a pitch call and then get distracted with messages and emails while the founder is presenting. But spending that quality 30 minutes with a founder with your full attention will help you ask more targeted questions instead of running through a checklist. This job comes with an inbuilt power dynamic and if we can't offer anything else, the least can we do is provide our undivided attention to a founder. Additionally, it's important to be approachable and timely. Use the "inbox zero" strategy and attempt to give a thoughtful reply to each founder that you pass on. Overtime word gets around, and your reputation is one of the only assets you have other than your network and your track record- in any case, ghosting a founder is unacceptable. Always try to keep the door open for future reconnects. When possible, end every founder call with valuable feedback, and be transparent with the timing/next steps in the IC process to reduce ambiguity.

2. Quick to the No

On numerous occasions, I get on a call with a founder, and in the first few minutes I realize that the company won't be a fit but instead of letting them present for 30 minutes and then giving them hope about possible next steps and a response in a week or so, I interrupt and am upfront about the lack of fit. I believe that any time a founder isn't spending talking to a relevant VC should be spent on building the business, so I give them the 20 minutes back in their day. However, after delivering the quick no, I do offer my time and resources to be helpful in other ways- relevant VC intros, customer/BD introductions, and intros to my portcos for possible synergies. To quote both my first boss in VC and *Moneyball*: "Would you rather get one shot in the head or five in the chest and bleed to death?" It's simple, don't waste a founder's time and effort.

3. Dig deeper

If you have the bandwidth to help, take the time to dive into a company that you're not actively in diligence with to learn more about its product, market, and fundraising strategy. Help them with those. Not only will the founders appreciate your no-strings-attached perspective as an investor, but you'll also learn about another industry and walk away with a strong connection in that industry who can help you source and diligence, as a subject matter expert, in the future.

If your friend is building a company, invest a small angel check in it. You will earn their trust. And as a friend, you might be helping them think through things anyway and if you're going to spend the time, might as well, participate in the upside.

All in all, be humble, have hunger, and continue to hustle. And don't forget to send the elevator down.

Day 2: **How to maintain relationships among VCs and Angels?**

Shomik Ghosh - Boldstart

A large part of a VC associate's job is to connect with other VCs (for potential co-investors at the same stage or later stage investors), angel investors (for potential help for founders and intros to new companies), and finally to know these various parties well enough so you can make qualified warm intros when the time is right.

Meeting Other VCs

This is perhaps the easiest part to do. Once you announce a new job at a fund, many other VCs will naturally reach out to connect. This is a great way to kickstart your network. Be open to these intros and and approach them with the intention of building a long-term relationship—not from a transactional standpoint.. These first intros will lead to invitations to happy hours, Slack groups like EVCA, dinners, and intros to other funds that may have similar focus areas.

In general, the VC associate pool all like to connect with each other. Most respond to requests on LinkedIn and DMs on Twitter. They are also open to intros from others that they know. So if you are not getting lots of inbound requests, you may have to take a proactive outbound focus. Don't be afraid to do this! If you do make an outbound request, always remember to keep info in as succinctly as possible. Why are you reaching out, where do you work, why would it be beneficial for both of you to connect? You have 300 words to use on a LinkedIn connection request…use them wisely.

Meeting Angel Investors

Angel investors can be a bit harder to meet than other VCs. The reason is fairly simple, unlike VCs, angel investors have a day job. They are usually working full-time in a role that does not include investing in startups. So they are not able to spend as much time talking to other investors. However, at the same time they 1) want to help founders and 2) want access to great companies. This is where you can help!

The easiest way to meet angel investors is usually through intros from others or direct outbound. What's important to note is most angel investors are not motivated by the money. They are motivated by the ability to help founders, improve their own knowledge, and perhaps even learn what a startup is like. So when chatting with an angel, focus more on how they would like to help and then bring up anecdotes in your own portfolio where that would've changed the trajectory of a company. This is what will get angels more excited to be in future companies with you rather than just as a source of capital.

Lasting & Proactive Networking

Once you've done all the above, you're ready to start making mutually beneficial intros! Again since you've focused on actually getting to know people rather than just "trading deals", you can figure out who would get along with each other and make intros that last. When you make great intros, people remember for a long time and will make sure to pay you back with intros that are equally meaningful.

Quality is better than quantity here. Focus on making connections between folks that have shared interests, seem like their personalities will get along, or are just good people who should know each other! You don't need to wait for people to ask, but can also proactively offer up intros to people in your network. The more you do so with quality intros, the more they will think of you for the same. This compounds over time leading to a great group of close relationships that will outlast jobs and likely lead to fruitful business outcomes as well.

Day 3: **What are some practical steps to source beyond relationships?**

Paraj Mathur – Panoramic Ventures

Being a junior VC is like being in sales. Your role is to source high potential opportunities, that turn into investments, and eventually successful exits. Even if your primary role is deal support (like research, financial modeling etc.), sourcing is a valuable skill set to add to your arsenal as your progress in your venture career. By the end of your career, you are going to be evaluated on deals you have sourced and led, so it's a smart idea to build a solid sourcing foundation.

However, before we dive in, it is important to recognize that "successful" sourcing means different things at different firms. Some generalist firms like volume based sourcing – they want to see every deal that is out there. Other firms are very thesis specific – 3-6 month research into a particular thesis, culminating in identifying 3-5 potential investments. It is important to identify which philosophy your firm subscribes to during your first week.

Unlike other roles within venture, sourcing is not linear or discrete. It does not "begin" or "end" or "pause". It does not take vacations, or weekends off, and it is extremely time sensitive. In the absence of a solid system, it can quickly become scattered, and overwhelming. Let's dive into the building blocks of a solid sourcing system.

One key thing to remember – no-one can see every deal. Sometimes partners will email you deal announcements with comments like "why didn't we see this…". It's okay. it's important to understand that over $621B was deployed in 2021 and there is no way a single human (you) can possibly see every deal. But we can create a system so we see most of the good ones.

The Low Hanging Fruit - Media

Before you can create your own "proprietary" deal flow, you must start with the basics. High visibility deals that EVERYONE is seeing. That's the low hanging fruit and you have to make sure you see them too! To do this, you have to immerse yourself in the venture and tech media landscape. This means tracking company launches, fundraising announcements, big customer partnerships, and hiring spurts. Here are a few (sample) publications below, but over time feel free to curate and focus on only the most high value ones for you and your firm's strategy.

ww	Communities:	Tech Platforms:	Newsletters/Blogs:
• TechCrunch	• Slack	• Twitter	• Packy's Not Boring
• Venture Beat	• Confluence	• LinkedIn	• The Generalist
• The Information	• GenZ VC		• This Week in Fintech
• Bloomberg Business	• Discord		• Industry specific newsletter (example - VRARA, Play To Earn Online, Crypto Tonight etc.)
• WSJ	• GenZ Mafia		
• Business Insider			

As you parse through these, you are looking for momentum. Any signs that a company is making interesting progress. Signed a big contract with the NFL as a customer? Progress and will likely need capital to fulfill that contract. Going on a big sales and marketing hiring spree? Progress. Launched a new B2B product and looking for beta testers? Progress and will likely need capital to scale go-to-market in this new segment. In addition, funding announcements are the perfect top of funnel signal for the next round. When companies announce their seed round, in reality, the round happened 1-3 months ago and the company is likely 3-12 months away from their Series A. If you work at a Series A fund (usually defined as a fund that invests in a post product, post traction stage), you know it's the perfect time to reach out.

Thesis Sourcing

Okay, now that you have a baseline of deals you are reacting to, it's time to beef up proactive sourcing. You should allocate a few hours every week on proactive sourcing.

If your firm does not have a sophisticated way of tracking each partners' theses in a central location, a quick high value add activity for your first week might be to spend 30 mins with each partner and document their key investment theses for the next few quarters.

Armed with their theses, it's time to deep dive and find companies that fit. Usually your firm will have a Pitchbook, Crunchbase, or CapitalIQ subscription to help you with this. Create a short list of companies that fit both the thesis, and the investment stage (and geography, and any other investment parameters your firm might have) and start reaching out to them over email, Twitter, and LinkedIn (I have even had success reaching out on Instagram, but know your audience).

Here is a sample cold outreach email:

Hi [Insert Founder First Name],

I am [insert your first name] on the investment team at [insert fund name] – super excited about your progress at [insert company name]. Congrats on your recent announcement for xyz (find a recent catalyst for reaching out). I lead our crypto investments and digging around the space have really found a deep need for [insert company solution]. We are super deep in the crypto space and have a strong thesis that the future of work is around composable contributions across DAOs and really love your approach for simplifying access to DAO contributions. (1-2 sentences showing you know the space and have a thesis around it, as well as your sophistication around the company's solution – personalized and really makes you stand out)

I would love to chat about how we can help! [Insert 1-2 sentences around specific possible ways you can help OR companies in the space you have invested in and how you have helped them]

Are you available at [insert 2-3 specific time blocks so they can just say yes – dont make them do the work of picking time slots]. If not, be flexible around your schedule if you can suggest a few times.

If you don't work at a well known Tier 1 fund, it's helpful to add a short blurb about the fund so they don't have to google the fund. This blurb should include location, investment parameters, and check sizes + a publication link to an article about the fund.

The important thing here is tracking and following up. Often founders don't respond to your first email. My rule of thumb: follow up twice over email and once over a different medium like LinkedIn / Twitter. If no response, see if you can get an intro from someone in your network. Once you have exhausted all these options – time to move on. Remember - perseverance and personalization are competitive advantages in this industry (within reason) so don't be afraid to follow up.

Network Sourcing

Venture can be a lonely job. It over indexes on extroversion (constantly meeting new founders), but under indexes on true, deep friendships with folks who understand the grind of being a junior VC. It's important to seek out your tribe – other junior VCs in the industry – so you have a support system to lean on as you progress in your career. At the same time, these are the GPs of tomorrow and can be a great source of dealflow. Start reaching to junior investors at firms you admire and set up initial introductory calls in the first few months. It's important to view these as real relationships, not transactional conversations. It's easy to fall into this trap – we hop on zoom, I share a deal, you share a deal, and we hop off. It's important to build trust and optimize for real friendships. If your relationship succeeds on a personal level, you will automatically reap professional benefits. The best way to nurture this channel is through biweekly or monthly recurring calls where you discuss interesting theses, deals, and learnings.

This channel is for high quality, vetted deals. I have found it to be most effective in two ways: for co investing with other funds investing at the same stage as you, and for identifying the best performing portfolio companies at funds upstream from you (example - if you are at a Series A fund, talking to seed funds about which of their companies might be getting ready for a Series A).

Brand and Inbound

So far, we have covered reactive, and proactive outbound, and network based sourcing. If you think about Maslow's Hierarchy and try to apply it to sourcing, inbound sourcing would be akin to self actualization. It's the holy grail. If the best founders in the world just directly called you and asked you to invest – wouldn't that be fantastic?

How do you make it happen? Accessibility and personal brand.

Most legacy VCs are hard to reach. A quick and easy way to instantly stand out as a junior investor is to be accessible. Broadcast your email, respond to email inbound, open your Twitter DMs. Make it as easy as possible for founders to reach you. Whether or not you invest, increasing your accessibility is encouraging founders and entrepreneurship and helps build your brand. Of course, recognize that you are going to get a barrage of inbound of varying quality. But at this stage in your career, time and attention is your biggest competitive advantage. You don't have board obligations (yet), founders aren't constantly calling you for advice (yet), and you aren't negotiating legalese with lawyers (yet). Take advantage of this and be responsive over email and you will soon start to build trust within the founder community.

The second layer of building personal brand is learning in public. You are likely not an expert in any particular industry – but are interested in crypto, or SaaS, or AdTech. Start writing about it. Do research and share your findings. Interview founders and publish the interviews as blog posts or podcasts. Create content.

Admittedly, this is hard. It takes real time and dedication and most of us do it to varying degrees of success. However, as you write about particular topics and share it on the internet – you are manufacturing serendipity. A founder might read your article, like (or dislike) your opinion and reach out to discuss. Boom – you now have a new founder connection. Similarly, an investor might read your piece and introduce you to a founder they know. Either way, putting your thinking and learnings out in the world is a great way to build a brand and generate inbound.

Conclusion

Right in the beginning, I said being a junior VC is like being in sales. It's true. At the same time, VCs are in the services businesses. Our service is two-fold: we service our LPs by making them money, and we service our founders by giving them capital and expertise to help them build transformational businesses. You exist to be in service of your founders. Internalize this. Once you do, you will start seeing more success with your sourcing strategy.

These are some of different channels you might use to source. It's better to start as a generalist and see as many deals as possible so you can quickly learn a) what makes a good company, b) what makes a good deal/investment, and c) what makes a good deal/investment for your firm. Once you learn, you can start to prioritize and customize these channels according to what works best for you and your firm.

Day 4: **How to pitch yourself in 2 minutes**

James Hueston - Primetime Partners

So let's just be real. If you're reading this you are likely exceptionally ambitious, exceptionally talented, or some combination of both. You know that. Your parents know that, your friends know it, maybe even some colleagues and professors know it too.

Well guess what? *Nobody else does*, and nobody else in this world could give a damn who you are unless you give them a reason to. As a result, this is about how to give someone everything they need to know about you in as little time as possible, and no matter the situation, so that they always have a reason to respond and work with you. Put that ego aside, and let's convince everyone that you've actually earned said ego.

What matters most in a 2-minute work related pitch:

1. Who you are.

2. What you do.

3. What the place you work at is.

4. What the place you work at does.

5. Why the place you work at does what it does.

6. Why you are there.

Here is my quick and dirty general 2-minute elevator pitch:

1. *Hi, my name is James Hueston and I'm an early stage investor at Primetime Partners.*

2. *Prior to Primetime I was an early stage investor at NTTVC, a $500M stage agnostic, sector agnostic fund with NTT group as the single LP. Before that I served on the CEO's advisory board at Cinemark as well.*

3. *Primetime is an early stage VC fund investing solely in the best people and companies that better the lives of older adults and those that care for them.*

4. *We were founded by Abby Levy and Alan Patricof who cofounded Thrive Global with Arianna Huffington and APAX/ Greycroft respectively. We typically back founders from Pre-Seed to Series B with checks between $500K-$2.5M and we are flexible to lead, co-lead or follow on in rounds with no sharp elbows.*

   a. *About 70% of our deals are in healthcare and the other 30% fall across fintech, proptech, insurtech, consumer, etc.*

5. *We do this because we feel that everyone else is focused on making sure we live longer but nobody else is left behind to think about the ramifications of extending our lifespans 20+ years beyond what our current retirement based society can support.*

6. *I joined Primetime because we do think about those ramifications and we are investing in the solutions to mitigate them. Just like everyone else on my team, we have personally struggled with aging and its implications on our family and friends. We finally feel that enough is enough and we can do*

*a lot of good and make a lot of money to do even more good
by investing in this space.*

Now, something that you will notice is that within my quick and dirty
general pitch I did a lot of name dropping and figure dropping. I
hate it. It feels boastful and braggy and that's never been me. But
unfortunately if you're like me, you can't be. You *have to sing* your
own praises because nobody else will sing or notice yours as they're
too busy singing theirs.

Now don't just name or figure drop just to drop and try to impress.
Every single name and figure in my pitch has a very specific purpose
for being there to lend me additional credibility, encourage others to
find value in my time and resources, and figure out how to effectively
engage with me and mutually get me what I want as well.

1. NTTVC is a $500M fund.

   a. Shows I have been in venture for awhile and have worked
   with very reputable people investing large sums of money.

2. Cinemark CEO's advisory board.

   a. Shows I can handle high stress situations at large
   corporations and understand some about their strategy
   and how they operate.

3. Abby Levy and Alan Patricof

   a. These are my bosses, and two of the smartest, most
   accomplished, and most powerful people I have ever met
   in my life. If you don't know their names, you should, but
   if you do know either of their names when I drop them, it

helps lend me instant credibility that I am acting on behalf of them.

    i. Thrive Global and Arianna Huffington are added to provide some extra power alongside Abby's accomplishments as she is less well known than Alan.

    ii. Everyone in venture should know APAX or Greycroft and if you don't, well…

4. Every other stat provides context on my sector, stage, focus, what I want, and informs people how they can interact with me effectively.

Remember, every one of these two minute interactions is a quick opportunity for you and the other person to decide if you're worth spending more time with. It's okay if not, but you want to maximize your chances so you can maximize your own selectiveness when meeting others if they all want to meet you. The one thing *nobody* can get more of, and we all have to spend at the same rate is, time… Give them the most time back by making their decision to engage with you as easy and appealing as possible.

Once you have given your background and listened to theirs, ask expanding questions on the things they gave and answer expanding questions on the things you gave. If it seems like there is overlap, proceed to the next stage and see how we extend our general elevator pitch to every situation and go beyond just the first two-minutes.

How do we do that you might ask? Easy, just consider the below three questions.

1. How can the other person help you?

2. How can you help the other person?

3. Where are you looking to go in the future/what are the actionable next steps?

Still hard? Here is an example. We have some fictitious portfolio company that desperately needs to sell to more large health plans. You go to a networking event filled with health plan executives. How do you effectively navigate the event to maximize your time there?

1. All of the health plans can contract with my portfolio company to accelerate their business. I want to develop a strong enough relationship with these execs to get them to have ongoing conversations with my portcos to explore any mutually beneficial opportunities.

   a. Do not outright say this, *ever*. They know it implicitly and will find it extremely off putting if you air it openly. They hold the power here, not you.

2. It may not be obvious, but since our job is to be well connected and always researching, we can always be helpful. They are always looking for new innovative companies or ideas or groups to partner with that enable lower costs and better outcomes for their patients. You know this since you are at an event for this very thing, but you also know that's always what health plan executives want. So give them what they want.

   a. Bring up interesting companies you've been seeing that fit what they told you in their elevator pitch (doesn't always have to be portcos) in order to show them you have your finger on the pulse of innovation.

b. Bring up relevant articles or industry trends and get their opinion on them after giving yours.

c. Offer to connect them to other industry experts or executives you know that they might find interesting/ helpful.

　　i. You never know what might stick, so just throw good ideas at the wall and they'll respond to a few.

3. Then finally, exchange contact information, tell them your exact next steps, clarify theirs, and wish them an amazing rest of the event.

a. The follow up is one of the most important parts of the process, and one where I see people commonly fall off, so be sure to send that follow up note and take action on what was discussed.

So there. Now we not only know how to pitch ourselves in 2-minutes. We also know why it's important, and how to use those two minutes of connection to springboard to a longer conversation and actually get what we want while helping them get what they want.

Rising tides lift all boats, and closed mouths don't get fed. Always put yourself out there in a respectful way, approach any person with dignity and respect, and as an exciting opportunity to learn something new or meet a new friend/colleague. You never know who might surprise you, and you definitely never know who **you** might surprise.

Day 5: **How to filter deals and operate in unfamiliar sectors**

Lili Rogowsky – Atypical Ventures &
Maya Menon – SeedtoB Capital

Perhaps you've heard the advice to "only invest in what you know." As a new associate, you're unlikely to be a subject matter expert in every company you come across, yet you'll still need to make a judgement call. How, then, can you learn to validate a business without domain expertise?

Become a learning machine

You'll find that successful VCs come from a variety of professional backgrounds – a trait that adds immense value through multidisciplinary thinking. VCs endeavor to be intellectually invested and able to context switch on a dime.

Regardless of whether you have the relevant background or experience, it is important to practice intellectual humility and give founders the space to be the experts of their own domain. Ask questions, be open about it when you don't know or understand something, and use the opportunity to actively listen and learn. *Pay attention to whether you're speaking more than you're listening during a pitch meeting!*

The founding team will - and should - know more about the problem they are solving than you do, so have them guide your learning. Before a call, you may want to do some high level research on the sector, though you'll likely find the most value in reviewing the pitch deck and other relevant materials provided, flagging initial questions or concerns, and familiarizing yourself with the founding team's background. There will be more time for research if and when you decide that this is a deal worth pursuing.

You can look to the founders to distill the pitch into simple terms and cue the points you should spend the most time on to present a well-informed analysis to your team. This is also a useful assessment moment; a founder's ability to clearly articulate the value proposition is a strong indicator of their competence, readiness, and ability to sell.

Practice communication skills & build relationships

Early conversations with a founder are also about first impressions. This is an opportunity to start building a relationship, so strong communication is key. The best pitch meetings are often more collaborative conversations than formal presentations. Opting for free-flowing dialogue over a more scripted approach often reveals more genuine and valuable information.

When speaking with a founder, focus on both their words and their delivery. The subtext of a conversation will contain important indicators of future performance. For example, (and this is especially true at the early stage) the implementation of an idea will evolve throughout the life of a company, so try to understand how a founder thinks, not just their current beliefs, which will (and should) change over time. Essentially, look beyond what a founder has decided today and try to gauge how they might make decisions in the future, especially when faced with the inevitable challenges and successes along the way.

The relationship between a company and an investor is a long one, and it is important to consider how it may play out. Consider whether the conversation is easy and mutually enjoyable. Is this someone you would want to work with or work for? Do you look forward to spending more time with this team?

A framework for filtering

You can become an effective source for deal flow by providing key insights about the founder and opportunity you are looking at. An important part of your role is identifying companies that are *not* the right fit for your fund, shifting focus toward those that you want to spend more time exploring, and identifying clear reasoning for those decisions. This filtering process can be applied fairly consistently, whether or not you have deep knowledge of a sector, making it a valuable skill set to develop.

The primary goals of this framework are to empower you to: (1) ask better questions; (2) get better answers; and (3) make better (and faster) decisions. To illustrate these ideas, let's break down some common examples of early filters in the diligence process to see how they can be applied when evaluating: team, problem, solution and market.

Team

- **Key Insight:** Who are the founders at their core and why did they choose to take on the risk of building this company? What are founding team dynamics?

  - o **Ask:** Can you tell us more about how you got here? How did you meet? What made you decide to solve this problem together? What are the skills that each person brings to the table, and how does that give your team an unfair advantage? Is the founding team full-time or part-time?

o **Listen for:** Complementary skills, alignment and team chemistry. Whether the founding team has the risk appetite to see this through and clear incentives to ensure long-term commitment. Think about how the background and experience of the founders positions them to be able to execute on their roadmap. For example, understand if they will need to outsource core functions vs. being able to execute on their own.

- **Key Insight:** Are the founders coachable? Can they strike a balance between visionary leadership and the self-awareness to ask for and accept help?

o **Ask:** What support (beyond capital) are you looking for from your investors? What are the key risks to the business that cause you to lose sleep at night, and what might we be able to do to help?

o **Listen for:** An authentic understanding of the long-term relationship between founders and their investors and alignment with your firm's portfolio support style. This is a great opportunity to understand whether a founder has a realistic understanding of the obstacles their business is likely to face, and whether your fund is poised to help de-risk the business and support its growth. As an investor, you'll likely experience moments when you'll need to share transparent feedback with founders you've partnered with, and even your introductory call can provide an early read on how these conversations are likely to look after an investment.

Problem

- **Key Insight:** What is the problem this founder is trying to solve? Does the founder have a deep understanding of it? How significant is the pain point?

  o Ask: How did you identify or encounter this as an important problem? What does success look like to you?

  o **Listen for:** How the founder's experience may provide unique advantages or positioning to execute on their vision. Look for founders who are focused, highly curious and uniquely driven toward their goal. For example, if the sector is highly regulated, consider whether the founding team has previous experience navigating those hurdles.

- **Key Insight:** Who has this problem? How well does the team understand the customer profile? How do they plan to expand across customer segments in the mid- to long-term to drive venture-scale growth?

  o Ask: Who is your target customer today, and how (or why) might that change in the future (3, 5, 10 years from now)? How have you tested your hypothesis via early sales, pilots, or customer discovery? Can you share some examples of key use cases for your product or early deployments where you've been able to benchmark the value propositions for your customers?

  o **Listen for:** A deep understanding of the customer and their pain points, as well as a desire to continue to engage with them and iterate. Familiarity with the intended sales strategy can also be a strong indication of a realistic approach. For example, when selling to enterprise customers, look for founders who understand the process and timeline, including downstream funding needs and time to revenue.

Solution

- **Key Insight:** How much progress has been made to-date, and is the team poised to continue executing on their goals? How do they expect the product to evolve?

    o Ask: Can you walk me through the product's current functionality? Can you walk me through your product roadmap?

    o Listen For: A realistic product roadmap and an understanding of obstacles they may encounter as they build are key. Ensure the team is being clear about what their product can do today, as well as what it will be able to do in the near term. Transparency about progress is essential to forming a strong and trusting relationship.

- **Key Insight:** Are they building effectively and efficiently? What are the key technical risks? What are the key milestones they need to reach to generate revenue?

    o Ask: What is your technical approach? What has been tested or validated? What have you learned or changed your mind about since you began building? What is your technical roadmap to revenue and where are the bottlenecks?

o **Listen For:** A balance between ambitious goals and attainable targets. Consider whether the team is thinking far enough ahead, accurately assessing technical risk, and delivering clear communication around milestones. Assess whether technical development is being outsourced, and if they are relying heavily on external resources, dig into the team's ability to attract quality technical talent. Evaluate for an agile approach to building product, and one where the team is prioritizing product features that can generate early revenue.

Market Dynamics

- **Key Insight:** Who is trying to solve the same problem? Is the team realistically assessing the competitive landscape? Do they have a competitive advantage that would be hard to replicate?

  o **Ask:** Who do you consider your direct (or indirect) competitors? What are the key advantages of using your solution instead of an alternative?

  o **Listen for:** Awareness of obvious and less obvious competitive threats. While others may not be tackling the same problem in the same way, the team should show awareness that peers who are solving adjacent problems may still be competing for the same customer budgets. They should also be aware of incumbents in the space who can quickly build or acquire competitive solutions. Assess how the team discusses their competitors, and be wary of statements that dismiss or downplay their existence – be wary of statements like "we don't have competitors."

- **Key Insight:** What is an exit in this space most likely to look like (e.g. strategic acquisition, private equity acquisition, IPO)? What is a realistic exit multiple and timeline?

  o Ask: What are the key inflection points that you expect to create value for the business? What do comparable exits in this market look like? Who are examples of market leaders in this space?

  o **Listen For:** Whether the founder has exit expectations that align with the size and growth rate of the market, as well as historical trends within the sector. When citing examples of comparable exits, listen for awareness of the economics of their business model and how it compares to peers in the space. If they intend to create a net new market, look for clear rationale underlying any assumptions they have made.

In conclusion

There is no "one-size-fits-all" answer (or question!) when it comes to venture. You may opt to specialize and grow expertise in a specific domain or adopt a generalist approach, exploring a broader range of sectors. Various stages, verticals, funds, and general partners will take different approaches to qualifying opportunities and formulating investment criteria.

Developing your own filtering frameworks can serve as a foundation for evaluating deal flow and determining whether to advance a deal in the diligence process. Test them out as you screen opportunities, triage deal flow, and assess both qualitative and quantitative factors that signal a startup's potential, even in less familiar sectors. Over time, this will help you refine your process and sharpen your intuition as an investor.

WEEK 3

ART OF THE
FIRST CALL

Day 1: **How to pitch your fund/investment focus**

Andrew Kallick - Listen Ventures

It's a good idea to get a sense of your fund's 20-second elevator pitch as well as the 120-second first call pitch. Both pitches will be used frequently and will seem almost second nature to you once you've shared them a handful of times. It may seem superfluous, but it's a good idea to physically write/type them out and commit them to memory. That being said, they will change based on your audience and the context of the conversation. Committing them to memory will give you the ability to adapt them to the circumstances.

The 20-second elevator pitch is one you'll use at networking events, during quick call introductions, to set context for a conversation, and maybe even in an elevator. The most important aspects of this pitch are making it easy for the audience to understand who you are, what you do, and why they should care. Below is an example of a 20-second elevator pitch.

My name is Andrew Kallick and I'm an Investor at a venture capital fund called Listen Ventures. We're a $90 million fund based in Chicago and we invest in all things consumer. We look for products or technologies that are operating in environments with cultural shifts and we help those founders build great businesses that change people's lives.

You'll notice I answer the questions I posited above. I explain who I am, what I do, and why the audience should care. A third of a minute is not much time so the key is to be succinct and clear while still leaving an impression.

The two-minute pitch on your fund is one you'll use regularly during first calls with founders. This is your opportunity to do two important tasks. The first is to explain who you are, what you do, and why the audience should care (similar to the 20-second pitch). The second, more important one is to leave an impression that encourages the Founder to have a real conversation with you, an investor that if all things go well, would be a long term partner in helping the Founder grow his/her business. This pitch gives you the opportunity not only to share more context about your fund, but also to share more about yourself as a person (previous work experience, passions, interests, hobbies, family, etc.). My two-minute pitch sounds something along the lines of the following.

My name is Andrew Kallick and I'm a founder/operator first just like yourself. I built my first business about 6 years ago and launched my second about a year ago. First one was an art and charity platform that enabled influential people like musicians, athletes, and cultural icons to release art prints that raised money for good causes. The second one is a website for online shoppers to discover new brands to shop at. Both are in the retail/consumer sector and consumer is what I know and what I love.

I've been at Listen now for about a year. We're a $90 million fund based in the West Loop in Chicago and we invest in all things consumer. We look for products or technologies that are operating in environments with cultural shifts and we help those founders build great businesses that change people's lives.

We're currently deploying out of a $62 million vehicle and we're unlike most shops in that we have a convicted investing approach.

We typically like to invest anywhere from $1.5 – 4 million and like to lead rounds. We'll usually invest in Seed and Series A rounds, but for the right opportunity, we'll also consider other stages and we'll only write about 12 checks out of this fund. So unlike many funds that utilize a spray and pray approach, we take an alternative one and are true partners. There's a reason for this which is that we like to say we back and build the brands of tomorrow so when you get Listen dollars, you get all of Listen which includes our in-house brand team. These are the heroes at our fund and the team helps the brands we work with become the editorial authority in the space that the brand is operating in. We've done it time and time again with brands like Calm, the meditation app as well as Dame, the sexual wellness brand.

I'm excited to get to know you, hear your story, and see how we may be able to help you.

Again, you'll notice how I try to be a *real* person given that the power dynamic between Investors and Founders can sometimes be skewed or intimidating to Founders when in reality, both sides should be on a level playing field. Depending on the context of the conversation, it may also be helpful to include information about what excites you about the Founder, the company, the industry, etc.

Day 2: **How to assess Founders**

Kyle Perez – Foxe Capital

I'd be shocked if you hadn't heard / read this repeatedly by now in your preparation to join the VC world, but this industry truly is a people business. While assessing the product, business model, unit economics, market size, competition, and more are all highly relevant and necessary steps in diligence, we as investors are ultimately backing people to execute on their vision of how they see the future. The reality of realizing this potential is close to impossible - less than 1% of seed-stage companies go on to exit for more than $1bn, so naturally it takes some truly extraordinary people to pull off such outcomes.

The following should help serve as a guide to help you frame your thinking as you talk to founders and potentially do reference checks. I'll caveat this though with saying I'd highly recommend tweaking this to your liking - founder assessment is the most qualitative and subjective part of diligence so creating your own processes will be helpful here.

A Founder's Roles & Responsibilities

- Define the product strategy and overall vision for the company

- Execute on this vision on a daily basis

- Keep the company capitalized

- Hire top talent, decide how to compensate them, and make difficult but decisive decisions about when to let people go

With that established, let's break down each of those and talk about questions you can ask yourself to frame your thinking.

Product strategy and vision

- *How relevant is their prior experience? How well do they understand the status quo and what potential customers are truly looking for?*

  o Great founders tend to have first hand experience with the problem they are solving or are, at a minimum, extremely well versed in the problem they're addressing and where existing offerings come up short. While product iteration is always going to take place, founders ideally have a clear understanding of customer pain points and are building directly to solve them.

- *Do they have a well thought-through plan around what version two of the business looks like?*

  o As startups scale, they inevitably need to add products or expand distribution beyond their wedge product. Founders ideally have a clear path beyond the initial product they're launching. Of course, learning will take place along the way - having a granular plan of exactly how the company scales years into the future is simply unrealistic. That said, being able to communicate a compelling next step for the business and product offering is key.

- *Do they have a clear POV on what the industry at large should look like in the next 5-10 years?*

  o In a home run scenario, this business becomes a defining player in its space and becomes an essential element of how its industry operates. Founders should have a unique perspective on how their industry should evolve over time and how they can shape this ideal future. That said, a compelling grand vision for the business and industry at large is one that is still feasible if everything goes right. There is a fine line "between optimism and idealism".

Consistent execution

- *Is the founder someone who is willing to roll up their sleeves? Do they lead by example with their work ethic?* VC-backed startup life certainly is not for everyone. Many impressive founders, if working at larger enterprises, could have teams of individuals reporting to them who actually take on the day to day grunt work. As an early-stage founder, there is hardly anyone else to turn to. Further, establishing a culture of performance early on is critical, so demonstrating what he or she as a founder is willing to do goes a long way in terms of inspiring employees.

- *Do they have an ego? Are they open to being wrong? How do they react to being wrong?* Even the best founders don't have all the answers all the time. When things don't go according to plan, founders must make difficult choices, some of which may involve shifting gears and admitting that their initial thinking was off. Caring deeply about getting to the correct answer rather than being right is important.

- *Can they get the best out of their team? Can they communicate effectively and continue to unite people around a common goal? What do we think the Glassdoor reviews will look like for this founder?* Working for an early-stage startup is far from cushy and requires a fair amount of sacrifice. With the amount of ambiguity involved, founders need to demonstrate incredible leadership to ensure everyone is constantly pulling in the same direction.

- *How do they deal with a crisis? Is this someone I'd want steering the ship when things go south?* A wide range of ups and downs are all but inevitable for an early-stage startup. Founders must be able to deal with this stress effectively and sort out the correct way to remediate issues, all while keeping their team on track and motivated.

Keeping the company capitalized

- *Is this someone who can get other investors excited about what they're building? Is this someone you'd be excited to introduce everyone in your network to at the next round?* Early-stage funds are obviously highly dependent on funds at subsequent stages to continue backing their businesses. Ideally this founder can get a number of investors excited about what they're building.

- *Is this someone who overpromises and underdelivers, the opposite, or meets communicated expectations?* Obviously founders need to swing for the fences with their ambition but being lucid about what they can achieve in a given period of time is highly necessary in terms of managing burn. Further, VCs will take notes on their projected numbers and compare these to where they actually end up when chatting again down the road. Best to not be portrayed as an underperforming company.

Hiring and firing

- *Can they attract top talent and convince them to join? If I were to go work for a startup, would I want to work for them?* Founders ultimately have to convince their team to forego higher paying opportunities with potentially better lifestyles in the promise that what they're building can pay off massively someday. This requires being inspirational, as well as being someone who people will genuinely be excited to work with. While you as an investor don't need to be best friends with every founder you back, they should at least be people you deeply respect.

- *Can they be decisive and make tough decisions when hires aren't working out? Will they hold their team to a standard of excellence?* One of the worst mistakes founders can make is not firing someone in a key role fast enough when things aren't quite working out. The clock is always ticking between funding rounds, so waiting too long to make a change can be truly detrimental to a company's ability to hit milestones.

Hopefully this gives you some food for thought as you start joining calls. I'd also add that there's no better way to learn what good looks like than interacting with really strong founders. To that end, I'd highly recommend trying to find ways to interact with your portfolio's best founders to develop that understanding and recognition. More than happy to be a resource however possible as you get up to speed!

Day 3: **How to identify stellar founders**

Pratyush Buddiga – Susa Ventures

The most important job of an early-stage investor is to understand the quality of the person they're investing in. Founders are the lifeblood of a startup, the source of its vision and direction. No matter how good an idea is, the startup will likely fail if the person leading the company is not excellent.

Probably the hardest thing to accept or realize is that extraordinary people are rare. Most investors when they start out think that everyone they meet is great and want to fire a check into every company. Anyone with a decent resume (think: FAANG, good schools, etc.) is considered a strong founder. What you must remember is that these large tech companies employ hundreds of thousands of people and even top schools admit thousands of students each year. World-class, world-changing founders are significantly rarer than that.

You need to meet with many "good" founders to understand what an extraordinary founder is. They stand out, there's something different about them, there's something that uniquely spikes. To paraphrase a famous Supreme Court Justice, "I may not be able to define it…but I know it when I see it."

For some, it's storytelling and vision; for others, it's deep domain expertise; and for others, it's a sheer indomitable force of will where you know this person will move heaven and earth to make their company succeed. Whatever the person's particularly unique characteristic, it sticks out like a sore thumb. You walk away from the meeting buzzing, excited to help the founder in the world they're trying to create.

Meeting reps are critical to being able to differentiate the good from the great. I myself experienced this after joining a fund last May. Every first pitch I'd walk away thinking "Oh, that was pretty good, let's spend more time on this," before discussing with my teammates who had a much more critical take. Years of experience had given them a much higher bar for what an A+ founder and investment look like. An important caveat is that venture investors get things wrong a lot, but that's okay. In fact, that's part of our job. It's a power law game where the biggest swings drive success.

Lukewarm is the enemy of conviction. Investors often talk themselves into a bet that seems good because action feels better than inaction. There are many ways to rationalize a decision, but the more you have to talk yourself into something, the more likely you are to regret it.

Extraordinary outcomes are created by extraordinary people. Your job as an investor is to identify those people, but it'll take experience and time to get good at this. Meeting 50 B's to ultimately find the A is a key part of the learning experience along the way.

Day 4: **How to identify areas of due diligence?**

Sakib Jamal – Crossbeam Venture Partners

When looking at a company, even at the earliest stages, I always ask myself - *"what do I have to believe for this company to break out?"* and *"what are the series of steps required to verify / gain conviction in areas that are currently unknown?"* In other words, there are a series of specific questions that require credible and believable answers (or hypotheses) for, with each question at the right level of abstraction to come up with granular answers. By probing in the right, needle-moving areas, investors can expand a founder's thought process and often win competitive rounds as a result. In my experience, the best founders appreciate being pushed and want to work with investors who do the work to gain high conviction in their pursuit.

Once the right questions are set, the framework attempts to assign certain probabilities or likelihood scores. For example, when underwriting a business that builds housing via backyard units or accessory dwelling units (ADUs) in California, one has to believe that homeowners will be OK giving up their backyard in order to generate an alternative source of income. The next step is to identify any secular trends (in this case, people are looking to pay off their mortgages or earn additional income), comparable situations ('granny flats' are already being built where possible), regulatory tailwinds (State Bill 9 or HOME act) or other factors that may make this phenomenon more or less likely.

Take another example - this one is a boot-strapped home services business, pivoting into a recurring service fee model to provide 24/7 in-demand service - raising venture funding for the first time. Here, the 'have to believes' are that the company:

1. Will be able to convert existing customers to a recurring SaaS model with low churn (<x%)

2. They can then change their operational makeup to dispatch quickly and on-demand

3. That utilization will be low enough where they can still earn enough profits after servicing

4. They can increase net dollar retention (NDR) by adding or bundling other services

5. They can attain insurance policies to backstop any sudden increase in demands

6. That the founder understands and is willing to take on an exponential outcome expected in a VC-backed company vs. a bootstrapped one

There are likely way more, but let's assume the first four points are all you need to prove in order to raise the next round of funding. Let's also assume each of these have a 60% chance - so slightly better than a toss up / 50-50 scenario - of happening between now and the next round.

Here's the catch: 60% to the power of 4 is only ~13%. That's not a high conviction bet – at that point it is it is 'hoping' it would work. One needs to take all investment decisions as far along the spectrum of a 'hopefully' to a 'probably' by moving as many of the 60% chances to higher levels.

As venture investors, the whole point of due diligence is to go out and learn more on each step identified earlier. These questions/ steps are the areas of DD you need to focus on. By gathering information from various sources including statistics, calls, and other forms of unstructured data, the goal is to move those probabilities as close to 100% as possible. If you do not have sufficient evidence, and therefore lack confidence in these steps, it is difficult to make the case for a sound investment decision. A common mistake is to confirm biases (everyone wants to get a deal done!) vs. objectively evaluating an opportunity — try to remain intellectually honest — call out and size risks appropriately.

The last piece of the puzzle is the rate of change – or what are often called 'feedback loops'. Even if you have conviction in all your 'have to believe' points, it may not materialize fast enough before your next round. So it is important to not only underwrite the *what*, but also the *when*. As seed investors, there is some leeway i.e. punt some of the 'have to believes' to a later-stage round, but it is still important to understand what factors are important to materialize before a Series A / growth round. At the end of seed round runway, even if current investors and founders think the KPIs are enough / or can be met in a few incremental months, the growth equity market may not recognize it and hold a high bar. Although John Maynard Keynes's quote, *"markets can remain irrational longer than you can remain solvent"* was for mature asset classes / macroeconomics, I'm convinced it still matters in startup investing.

Day 5: **Tracking opportunities / learning how to talk about deals with others**

Will Shao – CoVenture

Once you're convinced that you found a great company and are in the process of investing, congratulations! Now, one of the most difficult but best ways of checking if you're right is talking with others.

Speaking about the deal with others is a great way to pressure test the deal because

1. you're afraid of sounding dumb so it forces you to cover your bases

2. other people know more than you and will give you other viewpoints

3. once you are able to defend the deal, it probably means that you can pitch it to investors

So how do you formulate all your thoughts and conversations into succinct points?

My first step is to write a short memo. Writing always helps me collect and organize my thoughts. My short memos usually consist of the following sections:

- Background: how did we see the deal and how quickly are they looking to move?

- Terms: what is their target valuation and amount?

- Merits: what is good about the deal?

- Risks: what risks are we taking to earn the merits?

- Market Overview: how does the market look? What is the TAM and who are the competitors?

- Equity Backing: who currently backs the company and what is their plan for future fundraising?

- Others: What else does your audience want to know? Product, underwriting, flow of funds, etc.

Of these sections, the most important section is risks. The most important piece of learning I had in my first year was: your job as a junior member is to find and explain all the risks, while the Investment Committee's job is to decide whether to take those risks for the rewards. If the investment loses money because one of the risks comes true, it's on the IC because they were fully aware of the risks. If the investment loses money because of an unforeseen risk, it's on the junior member for not having thought of the risk.

Therefore, in all of your research and company conversations, always think about: how can we lose money?

Once you have all your thoughts in order, you'll talk to a variety of people: colleagues, IC members, experts in the industry, founders, your network, etc. Have a short, 30 second description "the company does XYZ to help solve ABC problem". Then, talk about what you think are the risks of the investment and the rewards.

Always keep your mind open, but provide your thoughts if you feel comfortable. You are trying to gather as many reactions as possible.

So talk with people that would give you genuine reactions, not just ones that are just trying to be nice.

And be intellectually honest. Yes, you are not graded based on the number of deals you passed on but rather the number of deals you executed, but being honest about the risks and merits of a deal wins you credibility with IC to do other deals. As Li Lu, a highly regarded value investor with close ties to Charlie Munger, said "Investing is about intellectual honesty. You want to know what you know. You want to know, mostly, what you don't know."

Ultimately, the more viewpoints you can gather the better. But once you find that you are able to defend your investment adequately, it's time to face the Investment Committee's questions.

WEEK 4
DUE DILIGENCE

Day 1: **How to think about Market Sizing**

Chelsea Zhang – Equal Ventures

As a former L.E.K. consultant (home of the mid-market commercial and vendor due diligence projects), I have sized more weird and niche markets than I care to count. IMO, the major difference of market sizing when evaluating early-stage opportunities is that, rather than getting to a super accurate market size, critical for mid-market PE opportunities to understand how much additional market share a potential target might be able to get within their 3-5 year holding period, it's more important to understand the market potential for a pre-seed / seed stage company.

Specifically, the marketing size exercise should get you:

- A good directional sense of what the TAM, SAM, and SOM, are

  o While having a massive TAM is always great, understanding what is near-term address with the current product / offering will change how you think about a company's 12-18 month growth trajectory and ability to raise follow-on fundraising, as a company will likely need to raise several rounds of additional capital to even sniff making a dent in the true TAM

- Comfort with the sensitivity of your marketing size analysis

  o Many VCs pass on opportunities because they underestimate the TAM, particularly for opportunities that are "market makers" like Airbnb and Uber where there are not great existing comparisons.

o A lot of times, you just won't have great data and will have to put in some reasonable plugs for assumptions so understanding the potential upside (and the downside) will be very helpful to think through the opportunity

Typically, I take the three-legged triangulation approach:

1. Bottoms-up where you do a volume X price build up to TAM

2. Tops-down where you find a topline number that encompasses the TAM but has other segments in there and make a series of cuts until you get to the TAM.

3. Secondary reports that simply report the TAM.

Let's use a straightforward market opportunity as an example - business-in-a-box software for beauty salons.

• Bottoms-up:

  o # of addressable hair salons in the U.S.

    • I typically leverage the US Census database for businesses to find the underlying number of businesses. This data is awesome and also classifies businesses by employment size, which allows you to further sub-segment into enterprise, mid-market and small businesses data

    • Oftentimes, this is where the TAM vs. SOM vs. SAM comes in - maybe only the small hair salons are addressable with the current product, but as the team builds more and more features, the bigger salons become addressable

- $ ACV per hair salon

  o If this is a SaaS model, you can apply a simple ACV per year that you think is reasonable (can leverage management forecast here if you buy the numbers)

  o If this is an alternative model such as payments or other embedding financing play, then you can make some high-level assumptions on total payment volume and potential take-rates

  o Similarly, ACV can increase over time as more features or products are offered, which is the difference from SOM to TAM

- Tops-up:

  o $ going through addressable hair salons in the U.S.:

    - the Census database has $ receipts, which is a good proxy for spend through through all addressable hair salons

- % of $ that is addressable:

  o If this is a SaaS model, can likely make some high level assumptions on % of topline revenue salons will spend on IT (likely low)

  o If an alternative model such as payments, this method might be better since you would be starting with a more accurate view of total payment volume going through the segment

- Secondary reports:

  o IBIS is pretty comprehensive and while not the most accurate, can at least give you another data point

The three methods **should** get you different results but getting at least three data points should give you a good sense of what the magnitude of the TAM is (<$1B, $1-10B, $10B+). In addition, using the above example, the assumptions I'd personally test sensitivity around would be bottoms-up: $ ACV per salon and tops-up: % of $ that is addressable. Creating a sensitivity table and seeing how flexing those assumptions up or down changes the TAM will also give you a good sense of the degree of risk that you might be underwriting. If the assumption that you are the MOST uncertain about changes your TAM by 10x, then you better go back into the market and try to get more clarity and conviction around those assumptions!

My personal view on market sizing is that it's totally okay to have fewer than three methods! The purpose of having more data points is to increase conviction - if you have two awesome methods, or even one that you feel rock solid about, that's ok if it hits the bar for whatever questions you and your fund have around the market opportunity. You can also incorporate elements of one into another - I've definitely taken a topline IBIS report and then applied a % for the segment of the market that was addressable. Last thing I'll mention is be creative! Public companies financials / 10-Ks, conversations with research analytics & industry experts, sources cited in decks, company websites can all be great resources. I personally really enjoy brainstorming on market sizing, so always happy to be a resource as well! :)

Day 2: **How to Approach Competitive Analysis**

Charlie Liao – Acrew Capital

Competitive landscape is a critical piece of deal diligence at the early stage - but there usually isn't a wealth of data to work with. It's also a tricky thought exercise - the lack of competitors can suggest both a true greenfield opportunity or imply that there is nothing valuable to see. Depending on stage (e.g., if more on Seed to Series B), healthy competition is positive. This implies a healthy market dynamic - you definitely want indications of demand. And classically speaking, competition drives better performance and innovation! Felt that was an obligatory comment because our industry likes to speak in truisms sometimes.

We look at three things - team, product and GTM velocity. Team is the most important element because it helps you get comfortable around open questions around the business. We care about the ability of the CEO to manage and lead (and even to maintain a public presence), the technical talent's ability to invent and build something truly differentiated and the GTM function's ability to aggressively and efficiently sell. It's quite prosaic, but finding the right combination of talent is hard. Product is equally as important, though a lot harder to figure out from the outside looking in. You can try to glean as much as you can from websites, but it's probably better to backchannel and learn more (ethically please!). Personally, I would suggest reading a lot in your spare time and developing theses you want to chase down. So you can meet several companies in a market map and then make a more informed decision much later down the line. We also look into available traction data, fundraising history and any detail around business model & GTM mechanics. This is obviously much more opaque, but helpful to dig for to make an informed decision.

Important factors to evaluate when you're trying to understand the competitive landscape of an early-stage startup you're diligencing:

- Easier to evaluate externally

  o Team

  o Product

  o Fundraising history

- Opaque looking from outside in

  o Traction

  o Business model

  o GTM strategy

We typically boil the ocean to find out what's going on with competition, so we'll:

- Try to meet with the relevant competitive landscape before any rounds kick off

- Crawl through LinkedIn / Personal Websites

- Backchannel with subject matter experts, founders and investors (Tegus is a great way to do this through their expert call transcripts)

- Read through industry reports / white papers

- Crawl through other social media (e.g., dig through Twitter, Reddit, etc)

- Read all relevant press reports / releases; reference old thesis work / company meetings

It's also helpful to identify not just direct competitors, but anyone who could encroach on the topline or mindshare of your potential investment. We typically place these companies on a matrix and rate the risk level from low to high:

- Direct competitors: Described as is - other startups who do exactly, or very similar, things

- Adjacent competitors: Startups playing on the margins - they may have an easy way to wedge over or have already started making early forays into your potential portco's world! Or maybe they offer a different modality that could be competitive

- Incumbens: ee the innovators dilemma

It feels like a tremendous amount of work, but once you start ramping on certain verticals the work pays off and builds on top of itself. Especially if you are sector focused.

Now zooming out a bit - as you've done all this work, you should have a strong sense of competitive saturation. If you've found dozens of competitors with little to no product differentiation, start asking some more questions... Otherwise, I think there is a legitimate opportunity. If there's no competition at all maybe you should think about the market fundamentals to begin with, but then again, maybe you're such a good investor that you've found the next FB.

Unfortunately, especially as deal timelines compress, it can be hard to do enough diligence on the competition before making the decision. This is why I've found thesis-led work to be helpful; meeting with a set of companies within a thesis statement (e.g., embedded lending companies) from outside the bounds of fundraising (or maybe from within) helps build the pattern recognition such that you'll have internalized what to look for in a competitive set. It's also helpful to build up an investor network with content expertise - I've learned a lot about competitive dynamics broadly (don't be unethical and poke around for MNPI) from idea dinners / conversations with other associates, principals and partners!

A few other notes:

- Everyone thinks that they are at the top right quadrant of their competitive matrix. This is almost always untrue. If you are starting out in venture, please don't take these at face value

- In newer markets, it's normal for founders to legitimately view themselves as the only players in the market. I wouldn't take this at face value nor would I view this as a dishonest statement

- Try to have a perspective on competition heading into your calls vs. just asking about who the competition is

- Avoid biases! There are some heuristics investors use with competitive analysis (i.e., overindexing on the competitions' investors or even judging based on website quality)

Day 3: **What are common metrics to look out for?**

Gabi Marques – Positive Sum VC

It's not uncommon to hear people say that venture capital investing is more of an art than a science, especially when investing in the earliest stage of a company's development, where they may not even have revenue yet. While there is some truth to this saying, metrics provide an objective and quantifiable way to evaluate companies' strategies, products, and processes. They also allow for comparisons over time or between different companies and scenarios.

This chapter aims to help you learn how to find metrics, identify the ones that matter, and, most importantly, make sense of them.

Metrics that Matter

Our first instinct when asked which metrics matter most and should always be tracked is to create a short list that can be applied to any company. If I had to create such a list of broader business metrics that are always relevant to check, it would probably look something like this:

- Absolute Revenue

- Growth Metrics

- Gross Margins

- CAC (Customer Acquisition Cost)

- LTV (Customer Lifetime Value)

- Run Rate

- Burn

There is certainly value in tracking the metrics on that list, but soon you will realize that the most informative and insightful metrics are likely not limited to that list alone. Instead, the metrics that matter will vary by company, and attempting to find a universal set of metrics for all companies to make decisions will likely be misguided.

*It's important to analyze metrics in the right **context***

How to Go About It

So, how should we go about putting metrics in context?

I believe there are two key steps to achieving this goal. The first step is to narrow your approach and focus your attention. The more specific your approach, the more effective your analysis will be. Tailor your metrics to industry dynamics, market characteristics, revenue models, or any other factor that you think makes the most sense. The second step, which is even more important than knowing which metrics to look at, is knowing how to prioritize and interpret them.

> **"If the metrics you are looking at aren't useful in optimizing your strategy - stop looking at them." -* Mark Twain

Go Narrow

There are several ways to narrow your approach to selecting which metrics to track. Given that not all metrics hold equal value, and it is essential to focus only on those that have the most significant impact on a company's success and strategy. Here are some ways you could go about it:

- **By Industry:** Different industries have different nuances and market dynamics, and therefore, some metrics are more relevant than others. For instance, SaaS companies may focus on MRR (Monthly Recurring Revenue), ARR (Annual Recurring Revenue), and CAC, while Ecommerce businesses may prioritize conversion rate and average order value. Manufacturing businesses, on the other hand, may index more on COGS (Cost of Goods Sold) or inventory turnover.

- **By Revenue Model:** Companies have different methods of delivering value to their customers. Metrics that are important for one revenue model might not be as relevant for others. For example, subscription businesses might focus on tracking metrics like ARPU (Average Revenue Per User), conversion ratio (e.g., trial to purchase), and churn. Marketplaces, on the other hand, might optimize for metrics such as average transaction amount, number of monthly transactions, and commission percentage.

- **By Company Stage:** Companies at different fundraising stages will have different milestones and levels of traction. A great ARR for a seed company may not be considered great for a Series B company. The table below has a few examples and metrics benchmarks by company stage.

	Seed	Series A	Series B
ARR	Can they get to a meaningful # in a good amount of time?	$1M	$5M minimum, ideally $10M
Revenue Growth	Some kind of growth rate that shows value is being created for customers (not necessarily revenue - e.g., usage metrics)	Doubling or tripling revenue every year	Doubling or tripling revenue every year *(Knowing that is natural for growth to decay over time.)*
Margins	Usually have lower margins, not much scale yet. So the question is if you think they will have high margins over time	80-85%	80-85%
# of Customers	Enough customers to talk to and understand why they like the product	No less than 3 Should be several, enough to verify there's a market.	10+ But range is huge depending on business model.
Run Rate	24+ months Assuming there are still things to figure out, good to have breathing room	24 months Raising to get to 24-month goals	Gets more sensitive over time

Go Deep

The second step is to truly understand the meaning of the metrics you have decided to track; going a level deeper and understanding what lies behind the pure numbers. For example, when you look at a company's reported churn, you should always ask yourself why the churn number is what it is. Which customers are churning and why? A high churn of customers that are not important to your business or not part of your key ICP (Ideal Customer Profile) may not be as bad as a low churn of your key customers.

It is also important to keep in mind that almost every metric is better understood when seen in relation to others. For example, you may have 100% revenue growth, but if it is all from lower margin products than before, or you have strong Net Revenue Retention (NRR) but a dwindling pipeline, it may not be a positive development.

The art of understanding metrics is also about turning numbers into **actionable** insights. This perspective can help you avoid the trap of wasting time on *vanity metrics.*

It's easy to fall into the trap of tracking vanity metrics because they tend to feel good. However, these metrics are basic quantitative numbers that reflect non-time-bound activities. They are not actionable nor informative, and are loosely tied to key activities, or not tied at all.

Instead, you should focus on actionable metrics. These are clearly defined metrics that measure performance changes over time, influence organizational success, and aid decision-making. They measure accomplishments rather than just work done, and are best expressed as a percentage, ratio, or average.

Some examples in the chart below:

vanity metrics	actionable metrics
# of followers	actual engagement
# of subscribers	opt-in rates
total money spent on marketing	ROI (return on investment)
page views	conversion rates
total acquired customers	customer acquisition costs

An Example: SaaS Metrics

Illustrated in the image below is an example of how to not only identify metrics that matter for a specific type of business (in this case Software-as-a-Service), but also know how to interpret them and compare what you find with specific benchmarks.

The image below illustrates an example of how to identify metrics that matter for a specific type of business (in this case, Software-as-a-Service) and interpret them. It also shows how to compare your findings with specific benchmarks.

SAAS METRICS SUMMARY TABLE

	ARR	Net Dollar Retention	YoY Growth	Gross Margins	Quick Ratio	Magic Number	Payback Period	Rule of 40
GOOD INDICATOR OF	Product-Market-Fit	Performance over time	Growth Speed	Profitability	Growth Efficiency	Sales & Marketing Efficiency	Sales & Marketing Efficiency	Broader Business Sustainability
BENCHMARK	Series A: $1-3M Series B: $5M	100% +	Series A: 3x+ Series B: 2.5-3x+	75% +	> 4	> 1	< 12 months	> 40%

Benchmarks may vary depending on company stage and customer segment   Sources: SignalFire, Mosaic, Scale

Here is an explanation of what each of those metrics means:

- **Annual Recurring Revenue (ARR):** Indicator of product-market-fit and whether you're delivering value to customers. SaaS companies want to have ARR growth over time and demonstrate cash efficiency.

- **Net Dollar Retention:** Indicator of companies' performance over a period of time. Measures how much your revenue has grown or shrunk by factoring in customer expansion as well as negative churn and downgrades.

- **YoY Revenue Growth & T2D3:** Indicator of a business' profitability. Represents the percentage of revenue left after subtracting the costs to generate that revenue.

- **Gross Margins:** Indicator of a business' profitability. Represents the percentage of revenue left after subtracting the costs to generate that revenue.

- **Quick Ratio:** Indicator of whether a company is growing efficiently. Breaks out ARR by month or quarter into new, upsell, downsell, and churn and gives a view of new revenue growth and retention.

- **Magic Number: Indicator of sales & marketing efficiency. "For every dollar spent on acquiring new customers, how many dollars' worth of revenue are created?" Example:** If magic number = 1, company is spending $1 in S&M to generate an incremental recurring revenue of $1.

- **CAC Payback Period:** The inverse of the Magic Number. Helps understand how long it takes for a company to recuperate the cost of acquiring a customer.

- **Rule of 40:** Indicator of broader sustainability of the business. The RO40 suggests that the sum of YoY revenue growth rate and profitability margin should be equal to or greater than 40%.

Another Example: Consumer Subscription Apps Table

Knowing which metrics to look out for and how to interpret them is great. Comparing those with metrics from other companies in the space will make your analysis and understanding even better! Here's an example of what this could look like:

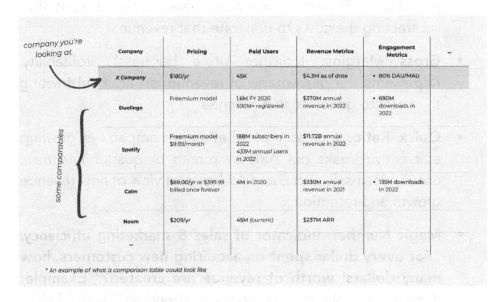

company you're looking at	Company	Pricing	Paid Users	Revenue Metrics	Engagement Metrics	...
→	X Company	$180/yr	45K	$4.3M as of date	• 80% DAU/MAU	
	Duolingo	Freemium model	1.6M FY 2020 500M+ registered	$370M annual revenue in 2022	• 690M downloads in 2022	
some comparables	Spotify	Freemium model $9.99/month	188M subscribers in 2022 433M annual users in 2022	$11.72B annual revenue in 2022		
	Calm	$69.00/yr or $399.99 billed once forever	4M in 2020	$330M annual revenue in 2021	• 135M downloads in 2022	
	Noom	$209/yr	45M (current)	$237M ARR		

An example of what a comparison table could look like

The ability to view different companies and comparables side-by-side provides perspective on the company of interest and makes benchmarks more intuitive.

How to find the metrics you're looking for

"Ok, Gabi, cool chart and table. Now **how and where** do I find the metrics for the companies I want?" Great question! Turns out that's the tricky part. While it may not be easy to get access to metrics for private companies and startups, there are a few tools and strategies that can help you gather the information you need.

You can always start by checking tools like Pitchbook (though you should know they are usually not as reliable as we would want them to be). I always add an internet search here or there, especially when I'm looking for metrics at larger companies for benchmarks.

The most reliable and unique way to go about it is to slowly build your own metrics database. One unfair advantage you will have as a VC investor is getting access to companies financial information (e.g., via datarooms) once you start talking to them/once they enter your deal pipeline. Founders will directly share with you metrics that are not usually available to the general public.

The most reliable and unique way to build a comprehensive metrics database is to build your own slowly over time. As a VC investor, you have an unfair advantage in accessing companies' financial information (e.g., via datarooms) once you start talking to them or once they enter your deal pipeline. Founders will often directly share metrics with you that are not usually available to the general public.

If you are building your own metrics database, make sure to **maintain confidentiality and keep it internal** *since most of the time, such metrics are considered confidential information. Alternatively, hide or avoid including company names in case of a data breach.*

Take full advantage of this opportunity. Take notes and keep track of as much data and information as possible from various sources. Although it requires additional work, it is undoubtedly well worth it. Over time, this will help you gain insights not only for analyzing deals, but also for conversing with other founders and fellow VC investors/associates.

Developing Intuition

Over time, with practice and repetition, you will begin to understand which metrics matter most for different companies and industries. You will be able to interpret them more effectively. Knowing which metrics to look out for will become increasingly second nature and intuitive. You may have already noticed this to be true for the GPs and senior investment members on your team. You will get there faster than you expect :)

Day 4: **What are common pitfalls in DD?**

Ryan Morgan – Crossbeam Venture Partners

Never forget that as VCs, we're here to invest in great founders and what they can build in the future. If you judge something based on their metrics to date, you'll miss the best companies. But at the same time, metrics can be a valuable tool in assessing which company has the potential to be a break out winner. Metrics - when combined with a pitch and interactions with the founders - can help tell a deeper story than a pitch. For example, high retention rates can help confirm that the product works. Lower CACs might help show that they have found a unique acquisition channel. But always remember that everything changes and the metrics of today =/= the metrics of tomorrow.

Depending on the startup, its stage and its sector, part of your job will be to identify what metrics matter, and how you can contextualize those metrics to decide if the company is exciting or not. One important thing to note is that you are looking at startups - not all metrics need to be "world class", and in fact the earlier you look at a company the less likely it is that traditional metrics matter. Because stage and sector matter so much here, the below general guidelines/ advice will focus on pre-seed or early seed stage startups.

In general, the earlier the company is, the less you should focus on any existing metrics. At every stage of a company's life you are investing in what they are building (vs what they have created), and for pre-seed deals whatever they have accomplished so far is unlikely to be impressive.

Furthermore, many founders (understandably) feel the need to show some form of metric to get investors excited about what they are building. While showing very early metrics is often well intentioned, be careful about how much weight you give to those metrics because they will certainly change.

Pitfall 1: Assuming anything about early conversions will translate longer term: In the first few months of your career, you will hear something along the lines of "we have a 12% conversion rate (for consumer startups)" or "100% of our initial beta customers have converted to paying customers (for B2B)." These are both great to hear, but do watch out for jumping to any conclusions from these statements. Just like early sign ups, it is safe to assume that consumer startups will start by targeting small niche customer sets and it is also safe to assume that enterprise startups will often target customers they know either personally or through a friend/advisor.

Pitfall 2: LOIs, contracts that should close next quarter, verbal agreements, sign ups, waitlists and all other equivalents may show promise, but should be treated with extreme caution: It's not real until cash is wired. I often see early stage startups show metrics around signups or user acquisition - e.g. "just through word of mouth we now have 400 people on the waitlist." Statements like these can lead to dangerous leaps of faith for junior VCs because 1) you may jump incorrectly to the conclusion that this means the product is in high demand 2) you may also incorrectly assume that these 400 or some reasonable portion thereof will convert into paying customers and 3) even worse, you may incorrectly assume that they will be able to scale up even in the near term without paying for ads or acquisition.

That said, I do think that early waitlists/acquisitions or beta testers can help show how dedicated the founder is to building something large - and I love to see when founders can show serious hustle and creativity.

Likewise, many startups tout potential customers that they are in "deep" conversations with. Good founders by nature need to be optimists, and most of the time they're telling their version of the story. But many contracts that founders think are almost certain to close do not. Invest based on the founders, the product, and their ability to execute.

Pitfall 3: Beware of thinking founder led sales can scale beyond the founder(s). You will certainly hear the following phrase in your first few months "Look at how many customers we acquired without a sales team - imagine what we could do with funding and a sales team". Sometimes, the founder(s) who says this is 100% correct - many early stage startups can benefit massively from an influx of capital and as a result hiring a full-time sales team. That said, one thing to ask when you hear this phrase is whether you think the founder is an incredible sales person and if so whether you think they will be able to replicate their sales magic with others.

Pitfall 4: Assuming that gross margin will be high at scale: Another common misconception is that gross margins at scale will be high - I often hear VCs state that SaaS is a great field because gross margins are ~80-90%. Many SaaS businesses like Snowflake actually have closer to 60% gross margins, and I'd argue that publicly traded SaaS companies have closer to 70% gross margins vs the ~85% that VC investors tend to believe. *See appendix for link to more information.*

Pitfall 5: Wow, look at this revenue growth. By nature, VCs are attracted to anything that grows fast - and often people shorten companies down to 1-2 liners such as "they're doing $1M run rate, and they're growing 5x y/y." While that may be true and in some cases very appealing, it is important to understand what drives the growth and whether it is healthy. At some point a few years ago, D2C (direct to consumer) startups realized that in order to get funding they had to 1) grow impressively quickly and 2) hit high revenue figures. Many VCs at the time had more SaaS oriented frameworks and if they heard someone grew from a $1M run rate to $10M in a year they were interested. Unfortunately, not all growth is healthy, and some startups sacrificed solid LTV/CACs to achieve that growth.

Day 5: **How to conduct customer interviews during due diligence + a template**

Jackson Bubala – Motivate VC

Customer diligence calls can reveal critical information about a startup's product, team, and market. Given the importance of this step in the diligence process, I've found it helpful to work from a structured guide to ensure we ask the right questions, avoid influencing responses, and allow for candid feedback that will help us, as investors, build perspective on the startup in question.

Customer interviews are exploratory diligence, not confirmatory diligence. The goal of customer interviews is *not* to confirm existing opinions. This may happen, of course, but your job as interviewer is to be an unbiased investigator. The goal of a customer interview *is* to understand:

- What kind of customer this is and if they're a representative of future customers

- Why they need the startup's product

- Who the decision makers and power users of the startup's product are

- How technology purchasing decisions are made

- How they found the startup and chose it over competitors

- The realized impact of the startup's product on their business (key metrics that demonstrate the product is working as intended, or not) and how the startup is measured/evaluated

- What they like/dislike about the product

- Their experience working with the founders

After uncovering this information, it's your job as the investor to contextualize it and interpret its impact on the long term prospects of the startup.

Here are a few more tips to ensure you elicit high quality information from your interview subjects and avoid bias:

- Get customers to tell stories

- Don't pitch. Investigate.

- Minimize leading and yes/no questions

- Minimize industry jargon

- 2 investors should attend every call. One asks questions and builds rapport, the other takes notes and can submit questions / flag topics to cover that may have been missed

And finally, here's an example template for running a customer interview:

Interview Guide Template (30 Minute)

1. **Intro (1 min)**

   a. Introduce yourself

b. Explain your relationship with the company and the purpose of the interview

c. *Optional, but recommended: Commit to keeping the subject's responses confidential, only to be shared internally at the firm and never with the startup.*

d. Let's jump in

2. **Background (6 mins)**

a. What does your company do?

b. What is your title and how long have you been with <customer company>?

i. Tell me a little about your prior expertise in this field...

1. How long have you worked in this field (finance, ops, etc)?

2. Which companies did you work for previously?

c. What are your key responsibilities at <customer company> and which team/department are you on?

d. What are your main customer segments?

i. What are the key lines of business or products?

e. How many employees are at <company>?

3. **Problem Space & Current State (10 mins)**

a. What did/do you hope to achieve by using <startup's> product?

b. What technology / processes did you use prior to <startup> to achieve said outcomes?

   i. Do you use:

     1. Manual processes or multiple tools stitched together?

     2. Similar but inferior tool compared to <startup's> product?

     3. No solution / workaround (i.e. this product was a total unknown until they stumbled across it / this product unlocks something that wasn't possible prior)

   ii. What do you like about these processes/tools?

   iii. What are the issues with current technology / processes?

   iv. How much do you pay for these tools?

   v. How many people support these tools?

c. Who at <customer company> makes technology purchasing decisions?

4. **Startup (12 mins)**

a. Discovery / Procurement

   i. How did you discover <startup>?

     1. For what reasons did you engage with them?

     2. Who made the decision to buy the product?

     3. Who bought/paid for the product?

4. Who outside of those first 3 people were involved (e.g. IT, security, etc)?

5. How long did this process take from first meeting to signed contract?

6. Which other products did you evaluate prior to choosing <startup>?

7. Why did <startup> win out over the other options?

b. Usage

  i. Who at <customer company> uses this product?

    1. What does this person/team use the product for?

      a. Was this person/team involved in the purchasing decision?

  ii. Which metrics do you track to evaluate the performance / impact of this product?

    1. How often do you review these metrics?

    2. What were your expectations of <startup's> impact on these metrics before using their product?

      a. How has the company performed on these metrics since using their product? Have they not met / met / exceeded expectations?

  iii. What do you like most about <startup's> product?

  iv. What do you dislike about <startup's> this product?

  v. If you could ask for any feature or change to the existing product, what would it be?

c. Miscellaneous

    i. Talk to me about your experience working with the founders / team…

        1. What do you like?

        2. What do you dislike?

    ii. If you had $50k to invest personally, would you invest in this company?

5. **Thank you (1 min)**

a. If we think of other questions or anything else comes up, do you mind if we reach back out via email?

MEMOS & WINNING BUY-IN INTERNALLY

Day 1: **How to build sector expertise: a primer on market maps**

Yuanling Yuan – Signalfire

The Value of Market Mapping

Most VC funds are generalist but it can be extremely valuable to set aside time to work on 1-2 market maps every year where you go deep in a sector. Market map exercises can help you increase your sourcing conversion rate as you establish unique insights that you can share with founders. If you publish your market map (see my SignalFire Creator Economy Market Map as an example), it can also establish you as a thought leader in the space, creating your own inbound and proprietary deal flow. Moreover, the exercise can help you create internal IC buy-in for a particular sector upfront and make any diligence process more efficient. When a relevant deal comes up in the sector, there is no need to debate the macro view, but only the company specific attributes. Keep in mind that the ultimate goal is to present your IC with 2 outputs: 1) key insights that inform your firm's macro views, and 2) a list of actionable investment opportunities.

Step 1: Identify Sector of Interest and Get IC Buy-In Before You Start

Start by shortlisting sectors that excites you or intrigues you. Unless it's a nascent space (i.e. Creator Economy, Web3, etc), it is much easier to dive into a sub-sector than cover the entire landscape (i.e. pick Healthcare Data & Analytics instead of Healthcare Technology).

Over time, you can build up towards an entire landscape but if you start with too wide of an aperture, you may get overwhelmed and not be able to complete the project in a reasonable amount of time. Before you start, run your sector ideas by your Partner(s) so you are aligned with what your firm needs. It's good practice to establish a mutually agreeable project timeline with your Partners because market mapping exercises can always fall to the wayside in the midst of active deals.

Step 2: Establish Foundational Understanding by Leveraging Existing Research

Now you have a sector identified, it's important to get up to speed on the basics. Look online for existing market maps, industry reports, opinion pieces or interviews by thought leaders (CEOs, prominent investors, etc). Here are some guiding questions for your research:

- Why is this sector attractive?

- What is the market size and growth rate?

- What are the major pain points for the different stakeholders in this space?

- What are the major trends (customer demand, product innovation, funding amounts, etc)

- Who are the incumbents (large public companies or large growth-stage companies) and what do they do? What are their business models?

Step 3: Generate Insights by Conducting Proprietary Research

This is the key step that will help drive you towards key insights. First, start by reviewing notes/decks on companies in the sector that your firm has spoken with. Talk to your colleagues who have spent time on relevant companies in the space. Second, reach out to your network of friends at other VC funds and ask if you could pick their brain on the space. Review their fund's portfolio (usually on their website or Crunchbase) and inquire about any portfolio companies in that space. Gather key data points on their investment thesis on those companies or the overall space. Finally, talk to any operators / advisors in the space whom you know or your firm knows. It never hurts to seek help from your colleagues' by asking, "I'm doing a deep dive on xyz space, do you know anyone I should talk to?" Chances are, your colleagues are very well networked individuals too! :)

Step 4: Use Data Tools to Filter for a Comprehensive Company List

By now you should have a bespoke list of companies in the space consisting of 1) large public companies, 2) large growth stage companies, 3) companies your firm has met with in the past, 4) your friends' portfolio companies and ones they've met with. This should already cover a vast majority of companies here but in the spirit of not missing anything, use data tools to do a final search on companies in the space backed by top VCs. Free tools include Crunchbase, Angellist, Linkedin and paid tools include Pitchbook, Tracxn, CBInsights.

Then, using the sourcing techniques described in earlier chapters, reach out to every company that you do not have any data points on that fits your firm's investment mandate. You should have a much easier time getting a meeting by sharing all the work you've done on the landscape and your unique insights on these companies.

Step 5: Synthesize and Present Your Findings

Everyone has their own style of summarizing content and company lists — Google Sheets, Google Doc, Airtable, Powerpoint, etc — it's really your choice. Remember that what your team really cares about are only 2 things: key insights that can help inform your firm's macro views, and a list of actionable investment opportunities. Make sure your findings are presented in a structured way. Be succinct and save all the granular details for Q&A. You should be proud of having done all this amazing work!

Step 6: Publish Findings Online (Optional)

Not everyone is comfortable with putting content out there and that's okay. If you want to give it a try or have a natural affinity for content marketing, it could be an excellent way to establish yourself and your firm as a thought leader in the space and generate inbound deal flow. If your firm does not have a blog or a firm-wide media account, go ahead and publish it on your own via Medium or Twitter!

Day 2: **How to demonstrate first principle thinking**

Jeremy Navarro – General Catalyst

It's important to remember that building conviction in a company is all about curiosity. As an investor, you should always strive to 1) assume you know nothing and 2) look beyond the face value of what's presented to you. You want to build as holistic a view of a company as possible, starting from its most fundamental assumptions (or 'first principles') — even the simplest facts or data points could be game changers. Then stress-test, stress-test, stress-test every assumption.

This is an essential part of any due diligence process. And if memos are meant to provide a holistic view of a company, then it's important that you reflect this thinking in the memos you write!

Here are a couple key themes or areas that I address in every memo to represent these first principles, and go beyond just product, market, and team:

The Thesis — In every memo, you should talk about the problem and solution, yes. I make sure to go one step deeper and also incorporate important context around the company's thesis. I break this down into several key components: the assumptions; the formula; and the vision. This framework helps show the 'how' and 'why' behind the company. Questions you might ask yourself to suss out this information include:

- *Why is the founder working on this problem? What assumptions did the founder make? Why did they make these assumptions? How did they find and validate that information? What assumption must be true for the company to succeed? Where do they believe the world is going?*

The Secret — By asking a founder why they started a project, you dive into *their* conviction and what convinced them to build the company. In doing so, you're trying to identify the 'secret' a founder has — what do they know that no one else knows? Often, these 'secrets' represent the secret sauce, competitive advantage, moat, etc. that set a company apart from the crowd. Questions you might ask include:

- *What do the founders know that no one else knows? How did they discover this secret? Why has no one else discovered this secret? What are the barriers to discovering this secret?*

The Key Risk — Every company will have a key risk or set of risks that you need to grapple with. Are you willing to take that risk and invest? This exercise, and representing these risks in your memo, can help you and your teammates better understand the key questions to incorporate in your investment calculus. Questions you might ask include:

- *What types of risks are at play with this company? Which risks can be overcome with excellent execution? What is the single, most important risk?*

Day 3: **How to structure investment memos**

Enco Wiener – Battery Ventures
Dawit Heck – Bain Capital

Purpose:

Investment memos serve as key repositories of the investment team's diligence, research, theses etc., and are crucial in formalizing the information needed to decide whether to invest in a given company. Most importantly, a memo (whether in PowerPoint or word document form) helps tell the story of a business, and what makes it a compelling investment opportunity for a given investment firm.

A good way to think about an investment memo is if someone with no prior knowledge of the given company reads the memo, they should have a good understanding of what the company does, what is the business model (how they make money), what market they operate (who are the customers they serve), why this company has unfair advantages to win, and ultimately why the deal team thinks it is a calculated investment.

Overall, an investment memo helps the deal team formalize their own thinking for how to properly present the opportunity to the partnership (or entire firm) in a clear, succinct matter; helps the rest of the investment firm understand the opportunity and come up with their own opinions, questions, comments and they also represent a source of record for a team's thoughts around a company to show prospective LPs performing diligence during fundraising.

Structure:

Each fund has a different method and process for evaluating an investment opportunity. When preparing investment memos, at times there can be both short-form (initial investment committee meeting) and long-form (final investment committee meeting) memos.

The correct length for a memo is a sufficient amount of information that helps properly present the opportunity at hand. In some instances for pre-seed and seed investments with little to no information, this can be as short as a few paragraphs in an email to a few pages in a word document. For Seed / Series A (depending on the amount of financial data/business metrics available) this can be several written pages and/or several pages describing the key fundamentals that help illustrate the company's growth, efficiency and path to profitability. For growth stage investments which typically involve larger check sizes and more information about the business historically (and trends on how it can perform in the future), memos tend to err on the side of including more information and data. Below is a recommended structure at a high-level that can be used across all memorandums. There are a consistent set of areas to cover, and depending on the deal architecture & certain questions/considerations on the opportunity, some areas may contain more information than others.

1. **Recommendation**: Quick paragraph on investment thesis/why this is a compelling opportunity.

   a. In these initial paragraphs , it typically serves as a summary for the rest of the memorandum and includes the key reasons why the opportunity is interesting (i.e., team, traction, technological differentiation, TAM, etc.).

2. **General Information**: Company website, location, number of employees, founder(s), investor(s), board of directors, company stage, company valuation, funding history, etc.

3. **Founder Background**: Detailed on the backgrounds of the founder(s) and the core executives. Deal team's perspective on why they are uniquely positioned to win, and color commentary from personal references of the executive team.

4. **Business Summary**: Description of the business, how/why it was founded, what problem it is solving etc. What is the current version of the product in the market and how do they plan to continue developing the current product (or build additional capabilities) in the future to maintain competitive differentiation and/or defensibility at scale while growing the amount of value they provide to a given customer

5. **Monetization Strategy & Unit Economics**: How the business makes money, its go-to-market strategy, what is the core ICP (ideal customer profile), customer acquisition costs, who are its current customers, what do margins look like etc. Unit economics are the core of how a business is working, it helps you understand down to a single transaction or how much a company earns from a customer in top line revenue, how much it costs to serve them, and what are the additional costs burdened to help them get in front of that customer (e.g. sales and marketing and customer success costs). The goal is to invest in businesses that are profitable, or will be profitable, on a per unit basis. This gives way to building an efficient engine that can produce cash flow in the future, if they are not already.

6. **Market Overview**: What market does the company operate in, how large is the market (TAM / SAM calculations), commentary

on the market, core competitors (+ funding history/investors in those companies) and why the company is differentiated. For market analysis companies can do bottoms up or tops down analyses to understand how big the potential opportunity is for the investment opportunity / company. Tops down include research reports on total spend in a given year while bottoms-up analyses assume a given amount of potential customers and what their likelihood to pay for the solution is. There is no right answer, it is an educated estimate. And in markets with tailwinds, these TAMs are sometimes larger than investors expect them to be. Or rather, great founders figure out ways to expand their TAM or SAM overtime.

7. **Founder Scorecard**: Ranking/commentary of founder(s) based on various metrics (specific to what the fund cares about i.e. technical/analytical ability, visionary, background etc.)

8. **Company Scorecard**: Ranking/commentary of the company based on various metrics (specific to what the fund cares about i.e. team, market, product, competition, traction etc.)

9. **Financial Snapshot**: High level summary snapshot (usually from your model) detailing financial KPIs like ARR/revenue, gross margin, number of paying customers, revenue and logo retention, operating expenses, burn rate etc.

10. **Assessment (Company & Investment Strengths/ Considerations)**: Key arguments for value prop/strengths of the business vs. potential risk factors

11. **Transaction Structure**: How much the fund is investing, SAFE cap/discount vs. priced round pre/post-money valuation, ownership etc.

12. **Further Questions**: Any other questions the IC wants answered that have now been answered/will be answered in the future.

13. **Investment Returns**: Description of assumptions used in the model and high level return metrics based on exit assumptions and different scenarios (i.e. gross proceeds, IRRs, MOICs etc.) In many instances these include sensitivity analyses to show multiple illustrative return profiles at different entry and exit multiples and/ different future growth rates of the business.

14. **Exit Opportunity**: How do we view the company's exit potential (i.e. acquisition via strategic/financial buyer or ability to be a public company etc.)

15. **Appendix**: Diligence information to include (i.e. customer calls, reference calls, additional market research, investor calls, etc.)

   Additional resources can be found on the supplemental links page.

Day 4: **How to prepare for Investment Committee**

J.P. Bowgen – Camber Creek

One could argue that successful venture capitalists are really just disguised salespeople. If you're not selling your firm to a founder, you're selling a founder or a deal to your firm. Your ability to clearly articulate and sell the value proposition that your firm or an investment opportunity provides will directly impact your ability to access competitive deals, and ultimately, your success in venture capital. However, I'd posit the most successful salespeople do one thing exceptionally well and better than most. They listen.

Pitching to an Investment Committee is no different. Your success pitching a prospective investment opportunity is as much about knowing the ins-and-outs of the startup you're pitching, as it is about listening to the question being asked of you. That sounds simple, right?

It's easier said than done.

Successfully navigating an Investment Committee requires active listening. Now, how do you know if you're actively listening?

Simple: you should be able to recite the question that was asked of you back to the committee member who asked it. In fact, as you tackle your first pitch, I would encourage all emerging venture capitalists to do exactly that. When asked a question, recite it back to the committee member. For example, if we play this out, a sample exchange could look like this:

- **Investment Committee Member:** "What are the company's primary customer acquisition channels?"

- **Emerging Venture Capitalist:** "If I heard the question correctly, you're asking about how the company acquires its customers and which channels are the most efficient channels for acquisition. Is that correct?"

Now, you'll notice two interesting nuances in the above exchange. First, they're actually asking two questions: (1) what channels does the company use to acquire its customers and (2) which ones are most efficient, as evidenced by the use of the word "primary." If you're able to listen actively, you should both repeat the question that was asked and answer the question beneath the question. In this case, the question beneath the question is: of the acquisition channels being used, which are the most efficient?

It's your choice how you choose to communicate "efficiency" – my opinion would be to rely on any quantifiable data you have to support your answer (e.g., CAC, LTV, cost per click, cost per lead, etc.).

Once you've mastered the art of active listening, there are really just 5 general rules of thumb to be aware of when pitching the Investment Committee.

1. Assume no one knows anything about the company. You should also assume that no one has read any material you circulated beforehand. In all cases, start your investment committee pitch with a 1-2 minute overview of the company and the opportunity. At the very least, at the end of your overview, everyone on the committee should (a) understand

the company's product and (b) understand the specifics of the deal, such as the amount being raised, your firm's ability to lead, co-lead, or follow, and how quickly the round is moving.

2. Expect the unexpected. More simply put, be prepared to go off script. Try as you might, the "script" you have in your head to pitch the committee will not go according to plan. Investment Committees are extremely complex theaters of human dynamics – committee members will or will not find the investment opportunity compelling for different reasons. This is where active listening becomes extremely valuable. As you pitch the opportunity, be conscious of the questions being asked of you, and by which Committee member. As you return to the Investment Committee for future opportunities, you'll start to recognize how members of the Committee individually evaluate opportunities based on their own preferences. This will help you mitigate the "unexpected" as you get more comfortable with pitching investment opportunities. Similar to how all venture capitalists should strive to build their "pattern recognition" muscle as they source and diligence startups, pitching Investment Committees is similarly about recognizing the patterns about how your team members think.

   a. Important to note: Just because you should expect the unexpected during the committee itself does not mean you should be unprepared. The evening before any committee, I extensively review the investment memo (or any company material) I previously circulated to understand 5 key buckets of information. These buckets, in my mind, are the foundational data points from which any venture investor should be able to get a quick read on the opportunity. As in, does this opportunity sound like a compelling investment?

i.   Product. What is the product and what does the company do?

ii. Traction. How quickly has the company grown month-over-month, what is the company's current ARR / revenue / run rate, and what is the company's gross margin?

iii. Defensibility. Why is the product in question hard to replicate and how could a competitor build a similar or alternative product?

iv. Team. Why is the team best positioned to lead this startup to a fund-returning exit?

v.   Deal. What are the expected deal dynamics, including valuation expectations, timing to close, and possible co-investors or syndicate investors?

3. Don't editorialize – communicate with facts. Respond to all questions you receive with facts and do not provide a leading narrative. More simply, do not try to steer the Committee in one direction versus another. If you're asked a question, respond succinctly – with 1-2 sentences – using quantifiable data you uncovered during your due diligence, and cite where the data comes from. A common mistake I see young venture capitalists make is something I call the "Notch on the Belt Syndrome." As in, in a venture capitalist's first Investment Committee, it's normal to want to fight for your deal, because it's your deal, and you want to get it done to establish a track record for yourself in the industry. If you ever feel yourself

falling for this syndrome, remember one thing: everyone on the Investment Committee is on your team. Everyone wins or loses together. You want to do the best deals, and if your first deal isn't the best, and it gets turned down by the Committee, that's okay. The committee is there to hold you to a high bar, and if that bar requires you to go to Committee 3 or 4 times before your first investment gets approved, you can rest assured that your first deal should be the highest quality of them all.

4. Take exhaustive notes. If you've made it to Investment Committee, good job – you've done 80% of the work toward getting an investment approved. You will undoubtedly be asked questions that you do not have the answer to. In such an event, take note of the question that was asked and who asked it. These questions can be considered "confirmatory due diligence" – or pieces of information that will keep the Investment Committee excited about the opportunity (should the answers to the questions be positive). Then, following Investment Committee, find the answers to those questions within the following 24-hours. It's important to keep up the momentum behind an Investment Committee to keep the team excited about the opportunity at hand. Once you've found the answer, respond to the Committee member via email, copying all members of the Investment Committee on your email for visibility.

5. Ask the Committee directly for next steps. Again, it's important to keep up momentum behind the opportunity at. At the end of your Investment Committee, ask the Committee directly what they suggest as next steps, and what it would take to get the Investment approved, so you have a clear roadmap toward getting your investment across the line.

It's important to remember that all venture capital funds structure their Investment Committees differently. Ultimately, the responsibility lies on you to understand the structure of your firm's Investment Committee so you can implement the above framework with the greatest efficacy. And again, remember, pitching the Investment Committee can often be more art than science – you'll have to navigate personalities, personal interests, deal dynamics, and more. However, I hope the framework provided above provides some structure to your Investment Committee pitches, and I'd welcome the opportunity to trade notes on tactics and strategies you find most helpful as you get more familiar with this key piece of the venture capitalist's playbook.

Day 5: **How to analyze and present data in an effective manner**

Gabriella Garcia – Two Sigma Ventures

As a former product manager, I have tried most negotiation tactics to try to get people on board with my opinions - building cross-functional personal relationships, highlighting concerning data points, crafting empathetic customer stories, etc.

Now as an investor, my job is the same, how do I structure my arguments such that others are aligned and we hopefully move forward with an investment. At its core, venture is a game of financial returns so fluffy or do-gooder pitches don't do well. In contrast to tech, in venture there is only one tactic that reigns supreme - data.

The Many Flavors of Data

There's many different types of data points that can make a pretty decent argument on whether to invest or not. These can include:

- Financials - P&L, projections, balance sheet, solid unit economics, great execution on sales / pipeline, low churn and increasing ACVs with customers, etc

- Product Usage - user retention across D30-60, time spent on product, number of users, etc

- Product Quality - speed x UX, infrastructure robustness, uptime, coverage, number of geos, funnel drop-offs across features, X additional features compared to competition, proof of expansion in teams/orgs, etc

- Respect or Virality - number of followers on twitter, activity across socials, number of GitHub forks / contributors, stars, reddit mentions and discussions, discord activity, quality of customers or users, number of app downloads and reviews across IOS (apple store) or Android (google app store), etc

- Market Opportunity - TAM, SAM, SOM, the market has to be big now and/or growing due to X reasons, remember we are trying to invest in companies that can hit at a minimum, a billion dollar valuation

Now let's dive into where you can find these data points

Meticulous Metrics

Money Metrics

Financials

The company should be providing these in a data room (a folder full of spreadsheets). I highly recommend making a copy of these within Google sheets and going ham with slices, cleanups, graph building etc. If the company is pre-rev or currently open-source (freemium) then evaluate the quality of their pilots, number of people on the platform, and their customer pipeline or user waiting list. For companies with a large user base, you are betting they can convert free users to paid so get those metrics!

Market Opportunity

*Jump to Week 4, Day 1 by Chelsea Zhang

Users Metrics

First let's define what a user is vs a customer

A customer is defined as the person/group who is paying you. A user is a person using the product. In subscription products, oftentimes there are multiple users associated with a single customer. Or people are users before they are customers. You need to separate the definition and language between these two things for teams to clearly act on them." — Brian Balfour, "Common Mistakes in Defining Metrics"[2]

A fundamental variable in calculating whether or not a startup's product is used, is by measuring "active users". However it's not clear what "active" means - is it the number of people who checked out the website, opened the app etc? I recommend using the main user action of the product as the activity event when measuring activity. For example:

Company	Business Type	Main user Action	Metric
Spotify	B2C free to use with ads	Listened to a song	Daily Active Users (DAU)
Medium	B2C free to use with ads	Read an article	Daily Active Users (DAU)
Instacart	B2C with one-off transactions	Completed an order	Daily Active Customers (DAC)

---

[4] To learn more, visit: https://brianbalfour.com/quick-takes/common-mistakes-defining-metrics

Company	Business Type	Main user Action	Metric
Uber / Lyft	B2C with one-off transactions	Took a ride	Daily Active Customers (DAC)
Zoom	B2B or B2C SaaS	Joined a meeting	Daily Active Paid Users (DAPU)
Zapier	B2B or B2C SaaS	Set up a Zap	Daily Active Paid Users (DAPU)

Product Usage

When I am digging into a company, I usually like to deep dive into product usage to investigate **three important questions**:

a) Does the product actually **solve the user's problem?**

b) Is it a **delightful and sticky user experience**?

c) Does the product drive a tangible, objective business outcome for the customer to justify the cost of the product (**the ROI**)?

Within product usage, you need to evaluate the breadth (trial to paying), depth (# features adopted to make them sticky) and frequency (easy to use and deriving value) of adoption. With usage, getting access to a Mixpanel[3] is essentially winning the lottery. If not, then make sure to craft a prioritized list of requested metrics, you want to be detail oriented but also not annoying with unnecessary asks as it usually requires them having to pull a few queries.

Specific product usage metrics are highly dependent on the type of company you are evaluating, for example, for a FinTech company, I

[5] To learn more, visit: https://mixpanel.com/blog/product-analytics-data-vc-investment-startup/

look at - average num of transactions per user, average transaction volume, total transaction num and volume, repayment rates, MoM GMV etc. Overall, you should ask the founder(s) for the key metrics they track (KPIs) and their north star metric[4].

For B2B facing products, I like to ask for:

- Activation rate - % of users complete the core action of the product

- Time to value (TTV) - time it takes for a new user to get the expected value from the product

- Onboarding engagement - time it takes to fully onboard, num of people who successfully onboard, self onboarding rates

- Feature usage - engagement across each of the product features

- Financial Success - monthly recurring revenue (MRR), average rev per user (ARPU), customer lifetime value (CLV), expansion MRR rate

- Customer KPIs - NPS score, satisfaction score, conversion from trial to paid

Retention - retention rates, cohort analysis[5], churn[6]

For consumer facing[7] products, I like to ask for:

---

6 To learn more, visit: https://future.com/north-star-metrics/
7 To learn more, visit: https://clevertap.com/blog/cohort-analysis/
8 To learn more, visit: https://www.lennysnewsletter.com/p/monthly-churn-benchmarks?utm_source=%2Fsearch%2Fmetric&utm_medium=reader2
9 To learn more, visit: https://www.lennysnewsletter.com/p/the-most-important-consumer-metrics?utm_source=%2Fsearch%2Fmetric&utm_medium=reader2

- Active Users - DAUs, MAUs

- Frequency - # of interactions per week or month, number of requests sent/received, impressions, activity across product features (one might be the wedge)

- Time share - time spent on the product (specifically active usage)

- Activation - signups, conversion from signup to X key action, funnel drop off rates between product features

- Stickiness - 30,60 and 90 day retention rates, DAU : MAU ratio

Differentiation Metrics

Michael Porter[8], one of the most cited authors in business and economics and generally seen as the godfather of business strategy, spent decades studying what it takes to build a durable business. He found that there are only two paths to winning a market:

1. **Operational effectiveness:** Performing activities *better* than rivals

2. **Differentiating:** Performing activities *differently*, or performing *different* activities, than rivals

You have to do it better or you have to do it differently. And even when you're doing great and beating your early rivals, you will still need to differentiate down the road. Your competition will learn from your success, copy you, and eat away at your margins. It becomes a race to the bottom. If you can instead run a different race, the competitive field becomes less crowded. This is why Etsy came back

---

[10] To learn more, visit: https://en.wikipedia.org/wiki/Michael_Porter

to its roots[9] after trying (and failing) to beat Amazon, how Airbnb (unique) and Booking.com[10] (cheapest) can both coexist, and why Apple continues to stay high-end[11] in spite of the huge low-end technology market.

Fortunately, there's many ways to differentiate a startup:

Differentiator	Examples
Be the cheapest	Walmart ✳ chime wish GEICO. Robinhood ✏ ARCO Booking.com
Be the highest quality	🍎 GUCCI ⓩzoom 🚗 WHOLE FOODS ♪♪ SUPERHUMAN 🔵PELOTON TESLA MasterClass
Be the most convenient	Uber ⑇twilio eaze 🔵turbotax. goPuff coinbase 🔹Figma 🔲DATADOG 💠Dropbox
Be the safest	🦆 DuckDuckGo ⚫ Signal ⭕vOLVO coinbase 🍎
Sell something proprietary	ⓐ airbnb NETFLIX cameo Etsy HIPCAMP
Make me feel great	TOMS patagonia NIKE IMPERFECT FOODS Stonyfield ORGANIC
Focus on a niche market	wish GOAT chime OnlyFans Etsy

LennysNewsletter.com

Source: Lenny's Newsletter

Now let's jump into some tangible metrics

---

11   To learn more, visit: https://www.nytimes.com/2017/11/25/business/etsy-josh-silverman.html

12   To learn more, visit: http://Booking.com

11   To learn more, visit: https://www.businessinsider.com/why-apple-wants-you-to-believe-it-is-a-luxury-goods-company-2015-3

Product Quality

Once again, this is highly specific to the company you are evaluating and usually has to be requested during or after a demo. I always do a demo with founders, even if it's just an MVP and ask for a detailed 6-12mo roadmap. You will learn these metrics over time as you see more startups, dive deeper into specific thesis and start developing your own knack for quality.

See below for some standard product development/quality KPIs

- Velocity - speed to ship a new feature

- Functionality - failure rates

- Stability - uptime

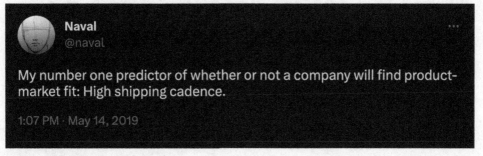

Naval
@naval

My number one predictor of whether or not a company will find product-market fit: High shipping cadence.

1:07 PM · May 14, 2019

Source: Twitter @navalravnikant

For example, if it's a FinTech company, I like to evaluate:

- Speed / uptime

- Currency / geo coverage

- Fraud / risk rates

- Data / security / compliance standards

- Delightful UX - do they have great clean screens, less clicks, intuitive workflows

- Feature-richness

Respect and/or Virality

Companies that know they're popular will usually be upfront with this data, if not you get to dig!

Virality

- Twitter - evaluate their presence on Twitter, are they getting good mentions, have high number of followers, posting often

- K Factor - the number of new users an existing user generates (greater than 1 is king)

- Viral cycle - average time from the registration of a user to the registration of a friend invited

- **Logos -** are the hottest startups and/or coolest folks using the product and talking about it

Respect

- From developers - search them on Reddit and review discussions by anonymous folks. Dive into their GitHub repository and see the number of contributors, forks and stars

- From consumers - if they have a mobile app, review both the Apple (IOS) and Google (Android) app stores, check out the number of downloads and read through the review. Treat it as if you were buying something on Amazon, you wouldn't buy a toothbrush with just 3 5-star reviews posted in 2019.

- **From experts -** review feedback on the company from expert calls, whether that's live or transcribed (ie via Tegus). If they are later stage, read through articles online

Data Storytelling

In today's data-driven world, storytelling with data is an essential skill for us in VC. But at the earliest stages in a startup's life, when there's often not enough data to extrapolate from, we as investors need to master the art of asking the right questions, knowing what to look out for in founders' answers and finding alternative sources of data to help us build our data stories.

It's not easy to craft data stories. It takes time to (1) find and (2) fine-tune the massive conglomeration of metrics above into a clear narrative that impacts each of your relevant stakeholders. Each memo is in essence a data story, a series of quantitative and qualitative data points - from team, product, market, financials etc. However, what is most important is the structure - providing context and meaning to data, thereby making it easier for audiences to understand and act upon. When you have data to back up your claims, you can provide a more detailed and nuanced understanding of the issue at hand. This, in turn, helps to build credibility and trust with your team, as they can see that your opinions are grounded in facts rather than just personal biases or assumptions.

You got this!

WEEK 6

TERM SHEET & DEAL STRUCTURING

Day 1: **Introduction to SAFEs**

Kwesi Acquay – Redpoint Ventures

Introduction to SAFEs: Part I

What is a SAFE?

SAFE stands for **Simple Agreement for Future Equity**: in this financing, the **founder receives cash *now*** but **SAFE investor shares will be converted *later*.** The price at which they are converted is driven by the price of future qualified financing, which is often the Series A priced round. SAFEs were introduced by Y Combinator in 2013.

- SAFEs are considered **unpriced convertible securities** because their price per share is not determined at the time of financing. A future financing round triggers the conversion of shares into equity.

- SAFEs are typically used in **angel and seed rounds**. Later stage financings (Series A onward) will include priced rounds (i.e. the founder receives cash *now*, and investor shares & ownership are determined *now* since price is set at time of financing)

SAFEs are **simple documents with fewer negotiation points than a priced round** (Example docs from YC <u>here</u>[12])

- The document's **simplicity increases deal speed and efficiency**

- **Primary SAFE negotiation points focus on dollar investment and valuation cap** (we'll come back to the latter point)

Please note as you assess deal agreements, it is important to have perspective from legal counsel as appropriate. This guide is not meant to substitute legal advice.

Types of SAFEs

There are many types of SAFEs that set parameters of what happens when SAFE investor shares convert upon Series A financing. **SAFE investor terms are focused on preserving ownership by influencing the specific price at which the SAFE shares convert (lower price = more shares and greater equity ownership)**

- **Uncapped SAFE:** SAFE investor shares convert at the same price per share as Series A investors' (*least favorable* to SAFE investors)

- **Uncapped SAFE with Most-Favored Nation Clause (MFN):** SAFE investor shares convert at the same price per share as Series A investors' but if additional SAFEs or convertible securities are issued later with better terms, the prior SAFE investor will automatically receive those better terms too; MFN clause will remain effective until conversion of SAFE shares at Series A financing

---

12 To learn more, visit: https://www.ycombinator.com/documents/

- **SAFE with valuation cap (most common):** SAFE investor shares convert at the lower of (i) pre-determined valuation cap and (ii) Series A price

- **SAFE with discount:** SAFE investor shares convert at a fixed, pre-determined discount to the Series A price (e.g. 20% discount to Series A price per share)

- **SAFE with both discount and valuation cap:** SAFE investors pay the lower of (i) pre-determined valuation cap and (ii) pre-determined discount to the Series A price (e.g. 20%)

What are key deal term trends for SAFE financings?

(1) 2021 SAFE financing deal term trends per <u>Wilson Sonsini Entrepreneurs Report</u>[13] *(% of deals that included following terms)*

- **SAFEs with valuation cap:** 86%

- **SAFEs with discount:** 45% (with median discount of 20%)

- **SAFEs with both discount and valuation cap:** 31%

- **SAFEs with MFN clause:** 15%

(2) Movement from pre-money to post-money SAFEs: In 2018, Y Combinator release a **post-money** SAFE to simplify ownership calculations for both investors and founders, particularly in situations where multiple SAFE financings create challenges in understanding true ownership before Series A round.

---

[13] To learn more, visit: https://www.wsgr.com/en/insights/full-year-2021-entrepreneurs-report.html

YC post-money definition (official guide <u>here</u>[14]) of a post-Money Valuation Cap is "post" all SAFE financings but still pre-Series A Equity Financing

- **Simple example:** If you have a $750k SAFE financing round with a $5m post-money valuation cap; you **already** know **post-other SAFE financings** but **pre-Series A financing you will at worst own 15% (750k/$5m)**

  - o **However, you will still have dilution from the Series A financing:** If Series A investors seek 20% post-money ownership, the SAFE investor post-Series A ownership will be (1-20%)*15%= 12% (i.e. since Series A has right to 20% post-money, our ownership is 15% of the remaining 80%).

    - **Practitioner note: If you hear "pre-money" or "post-money", ALWAYS consider what transactions are and aren't included, as it has serious implications on your view of ownership**

The National Venture Capital Association (NVCA) and select law firms publish helpful reports/resources that provide context on deal term trends

Please note every deal is its own situation, so "market terms" are not necessarily an indication of what terms "should" be in your deal every time; As mentioned, these resources are not a replacement for legal counsel.

- <u>NVCA term sheet (market benchmarks)</u>[15]

---

[14] To learn more, visit: https://www.ycombinator.com/assets/ycdc/Primer%20for%20post -money%20safe%20v1.1-2af8129e12effd9638eeab383b7309142c8f415e5cdb0bc210 d573f779177a1c.pdf

[15] To learn more, visit: https://www.aumni.fund/resources/enhanced-model-term- sheet?utm_source=NVCA&utm_medium=model-doc-homepage

- Wilson Sonsini Entrepreneurs Report[16]

- WilmerHale Venture Capital Report (market deal terms over time)[17]

Sources: Y Combinator, Wilson Sonsini, Wilmer Hale, Carta, DLA Piper, Cooley, Harvard Business School Entrepreneurial Finance course

Introduction to SAFEs: Part II

In Introduction to SAFEs Part I, we learned (i) what is a SAFE, (ii) types of SAFEs, and (iii) deal term trends for SAFEs.

Today, we will apply these concepts to take a quantitative view on how SAFEs convert on the cap table upon Series A financing. While early-stage investing has limited numbers, a junior investor's ability to lean into the math can be a competitive advantage.

Let's say you invested using a post-money SAFE: $750k with both a $5m post-money valuation cap and a 20% discount. We will leave employee option pools out of this exercise for simplicity (*option pools are shares that are reserved for employees. Depending on the terms, they can create more dilution and less ownership for founders and investors.*)

What do we know at the time of the SAFE deal?

- **Before any Series A financing, we know:**

  o The founder receives $750k

---

[16] To learn more, visit: https://www.wsgr.com/en/insights/full-year-2021-entrepreneurs-report.html

[17] To learn more, visit: https://www.wilmerhale.com/en/insights/publications/2021-venture-capital-report

o   Since this is a post-money SAFE (*remember post-all future SAFE financings, but pre-Series A financing*), our worst case ownership pre-Series A dilution will be 15% (750k / $5m)

- **What do we not know yet?**

  o   We don't know the Series A valuation yet. As a result it is:

    - **Unclear whether we will elect to use the $5m valuation cap or the 20% discount** to drive the price of our SAFE to the lower, investor specific price

    - **Unclear how many shares we will have (and thus our ownership percentage)** post-Series A financing

  - **A cap table reflection below:**

	Pre-Series A		Post-Series A		
	# shares	%	# shares	%	Price per share
Founders	1,000,000	100%	1,000,000	???	--
Series A Investor			???	???	???
SAFE Angel Investor			???	???	???
Total	1,000,000	100%	???	???	

Note: 1m founder shares are illustrative

To fill the post-Series A cap table, we will follow a three step process:

- **Step 1:** Calculate the Series A pre-money valuation

- **Step 2:** Based on Series A valuation, identify what price the SAFE shares convert at; We will calculate the price per share under both the post-money valuation cap and discount and choose the lower of the two (*lower price = higher ownership*)

- **Step 3:** Figure out ownership of the cap table accordingly to understand remaining ownership impact

Step 1: What is the pre-money Series A valuation?

- **We need to first figure out our pre-money Series A valuation to feed into our analysis of whether we will elect to use our valuation cap price or discounted price to convert our SAFE shares**

- **Let's lay out the Series A financing valuation terms:**

  o We will assume a **$4m financing** for **20% post-money ownership**

  o **What's our post-money valuation?** Amount invested / post-money ownership target → $4m invested / 20% post-money ownership target = **$20m post-money valuation**

  o What's our **pre-money valuation**? Post-money valuation minus amount invested → $20m post money valuation - $4m invested = **$16m pre-money valuation**

- **A cap table reflection below:** We now know that the Series A investor will have 20% post-money ownership. We still do not know the Series A price **per share** even though we have Series A valuation: we need to know the SAFE share conversion to know total number of shares ****

	Pre-Series A		Post-Series A		
	# shares	%	# shares	%	Price per share
Founders	1,000,000	100%	1,000,000	???	--
Series A Investor			???	20%	???
SAFE Angel Investor			???	???	???
Total	**1,000,000**	**100%**	**???**	**???**	

Step 2: What price will the SAFE shares convert at? What price will Series A shares convert at?

- Now that we have the Series A pre-money valuation, we need to determine which method, 20% discount or valuation cap, produces the lowest price per share for the SAFE investors

- On the accompanying Excel workbook (found on bit.ly/ YoungVCBookLinks - case sensitive), I do the following:

  o a) **Calculate the Pre-money valuation (pre-Series A, pre SAFE):** Post-money valuation - investment

  o b) **Calculate SAFE price per share:** Pre-money valuation / existing shares *(share for both pre-Series A and pre-SAFE investments)*

  o (c) **Determine SAFE shares upon conversion:** SAFE investment amount / SAFE price per share

What SAFE price do we get using a 20% discount?	
Series A pre-money valuation	$16,000,000
Discounted pre-money valuation (@ 20% discount)	$12,800,000
Less: SAFE investment	($750,000)
a) Pre-money valuation, pre-Series A, pre-SAFE note	$12,050,000
Existing shares (pre-SAFE note conversion, pre-Series A)	1,000,000
b) SAFE investor price per share @ discount	$12.05
c) Implied SAFE investor shares upon conversion	62,241
Series A price per share (if SAFE investor elects 20% discount)	$15.06
Series A shares (if SAFE investor elects 20% discount)	265,560

> Does the 20% discount or the valuation cap generate the *lowest price per share (highest share conversion)?*

What SAFE price do we get using a $5m post-money valuation cap?	
SAFE Valuation Cap (Post Money)	$5,000,000
Less: SAFE investment	($750,000)
a) Pre-money valuation, pre-Series A, pre-SAFE note	$4,250,000
Existing shares (pre-SAFE note conversion, pre-Series A)	1,000,000
(b) SAFE investor price per share @ valuation cap	$4.25
(c) Implied SAFE investor shares upon conversion	176,471
Series A price per share (if SAFE investor elects valuation cap)	$13.60
Series A shares (if SAFE investor elects valuation cap)	294,118

What's our preferred method? (approach that yields lowest SAFE price)	$5m post-money val. cap
(b) SAFE investor price per share @ valuation cap	$4.25
(c) Implied SAFE investor shares upon conversion	176,471
Implied Series A price per share	$13.60
Series A shares (if SAFE investor elects valuation cap)	294,118

- **We see that SAFE investors will elect for the post-money valuation cap over the discount. The valuation cap**

provides the lowest price per share ($4.25 vs. $12.05) and consequently the most shares (176,471 vs. 62,241).

- **Now that we know our SAFE conversion method, we also now know the Series A price per share and implied shares: $13.60 and 294,118**

- **We now have all our inputs to fill out our post-Series A cap table** *(again, don't worry about getting all the math now; I will provide the spreadsheet link so you can see step by step calculations and commentary)*

Step 3: What's our final cap table post-Series A?

- **We now know the SAFE investors will convert using the $5m valuation cap, and therefore:**

  o SAFE investor price per share and shares are **$4.25** and **176,471** respectively

  o Series A investor price per share and shares are **$13.60** and **294,118** respectively

- **The completed cap table, post-Series A is as follows:**

	Pre-Series A		Post-Series A		
	# shares	%	# shares	%	Price per share
Founders	1,000,000	100%	1,000,000	68%	--
Series A Investor			294,118	20%	$13.60
SAFE Angel Investor			176,471	12%	$4.25
Total	1,000,000	100%	1,470,588	100%	

Additional considerations: SAFE ownership under various terms

The following table is meant to illustrate how SAFE financing deal terms can impact ownership post-Series A. Having no discount or valuation cap means that SAFE investors convert at the higher Series A price (and thus have least amount of ownership). For the Series A valuation of $16m pre-money, we would prefer the $5m post-money valuation cap over the 20% discount.

SAFE ownership under various terms											
	Pre-Series A		Post-Series A								
			(a) No Discount, No valuation cap			(b) Discount			(c) Valuation cap		
	# shares	%	# shares	%	Price per share	# shares	%	Price per share	# shares	%	Price per share
Founders	1,000,000	100%	1,000,000	76%	--	1,000,000	75%	--	1,000,000	68%	--
Series A Investor			262,295	20%	$15.25	265,560	20%	$15.06	294,118	20%	$13.60
SAFE Angel Investor			49,180	4%	$15.25	62,241	5%	$12.05	176,471	12%	$4.25
Total	1,000,000	100%	1,311,475	100%		1,327,801	100%		1,470,588	100%	

- **No discount / no valuation cap (least favorable) |** SAFE investor converts at Series A price of $15.25/share; 4% ownership post-Series A

- **Discount (more favorable) |** SAFE investor converts at $12.05 /share (20% discount to Series A price); 5% ownership post-Series A

- **Valuation cap (most favorable) |** SAFE investor converts at $4.25 / share, 12% ownership post-Series A

Keep in mind, that the valuation cap is preferable at the example Series A pre-money valuation of $16m; As Series A valuation increases or decreases, your preferences to a discount vs. valuation cap may change.

Additional Discount vs. valuation cap preference under various valuation scenarios

- **The below table represents how a change in valuation can change SAFE investor preference to convert at either the**

$5m post-money valuation cap or 20% discount *(should deal terms provide option for both)*

o   At pre-money valuation **below $6.25m:** prefer 20% discount

o   At pre-money valuation **above $6.25m:** prefer $5m post-money cap

o   Note at high valuations, the valuation cap is most likely to protect SAFE investor ownership

o   Keep in mind the valuation cap dollar amount will change the nature of the below chart (e.g. $5m valuation cap → $10m valuation cap)

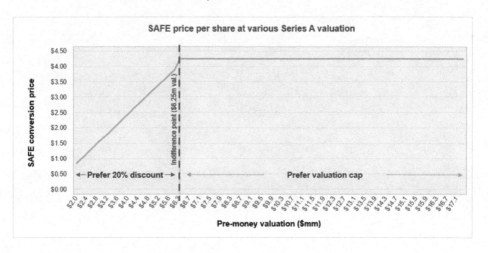

Conclusion and spreadsheet resource

If you want to dig into the math more, I have left the google spreadsheet here[18]

---

[18] To learn more, visit: https://docs.google.com/spreadsheets/d/1oGzP8cuua6L Giht9f1OMI_EFpdH3YPg4/edit?usp=sharing&ouid=115327217686289 772077&rtpof=true&sd=true

I hope you found this introduction to SAFEs informative as a useful guide to leverage along your VC journey. As previously mentioned, Part I and Part II are not meant to substitute legal counsel.

Sources: Y Combinator, Wilson Sonsini, Wilmer Hale, Carta, DLA Piper, Cooley, Harvard Business School Entrepreneurial Finance course

Day 2: **What are the basics of VC Math & Dilution**

Ian Goldberg - Venrex

This chapter includes an accompanying Excel workbook that can be found at bit.ly/YoungVCBookLinks

There are several qualified takes on venture math out there from the likes of <u>Fred Wilson</u>[19] and <u>Andrew Chen</u>[20]. Harlem Capital also put out a <u>great piece</u>[21] in 2020. The main takeaway is that a <u>power law exists in venture</u>[22], meaning that the bulk of returns for a successful fund are likely to come from a very small amount of deals in the portfolio...maybe just one. When underwriting an opportunity, an investor must have confidence that the company has a chance to provide an outsized return. Given the high likelihood of startup failure, the ones that go on to be extremely successful allow venture capitalists to go back to their LPs and justify raising additional funds in the future.

Let's look at a simple scenario -

- $50M seed fund

- $7M in management fees over lifecycle of fund

    o   (2% over 7 years - ignoring any recycling)

---

[19] To learn more, visit: https://avc.com/2008/08/venture-fund-ec/
[20] Visit: https://andrewchen.com/venture-capital-returns/
[21] Visit: https://medium.com/@harlemcapital/can-your-startup-return-the-fund-6e233bd5c8b2
[22] Visit: https://altos.vc/blog/paradox-of-the-power-law-in-venture-capital

- $43 of investable capital

- $21.5M reserved for follow-on capital (50% of capital)

- $1M avg initial check size

- 21 total companies in the fund

Assumptions:

- $2M/deal allocated equally
- 10 companies return $0
- 6 companies 1x ($12M x 1 = $12M)
- 2 companies 3x ($4M x 3 = $12M)
- 2 companies 10x ($4M x 10 = $40M)
- 1 company 50x ($2M x 50 = $100M)

Gross Return:

$164M (3.28x MOIC)

In this scenario with one fund returner, the 50x deal is responsible for 61% of gross proceeds. This percentage of total proceeds from one deal can be and has been much higher than 61% for certain funds (e.g. those early in Uber, Coinbase, Facebook).

Now, let's assume instead of the one portfolio company returning the fund with a 50x, that deal ends up being a 10x. What happens? Our gross return for the fund drops to 84M and a 1.7x multiple. Most seed stage firms target a 3x net of fees, which makes the 1.7x gross MOIC a tough pill to swallow. This also hits on the different incentives amongst founders and investors. The same 10x exit scenario which is a mediocre outcome for a VC might be a huge, successful outcome for a founder. But the math speaks for itself - if half of the companies in a venture fund's portfolio go to zero and the other half of companies 5 to 10x, the venture fund has not performed well (assuming equal $ weighting across each portfolio company).

The following quote from The Power Law[23], by Sebastian Mallaby, exemplifies the venture math dynamics: "In the two decades he (Vinod Khosla) spent at Kleiner Perkins before starting his own venture firm, he learned not to worry about the bets that went to zero. All he could lose was one times his money. What Khosla cared about were the bets that did pay off."

Note: 'not to worry' does not mean that you should not care about portfolio companies that are not performing well. This is strictly in the context of funds returns

Startup	Investment	Return	Multiple
Juniper Networks	$5M	$7B	1,400
Siara	A few $M	$1,5B	>150
Cerent	$8M	Bought for $7B	

VC Math Excel

The attached excel helps visualize outcome scenarios over the lifecycle of a company. It is impossible to perfectly project future cash needs, timing of such needs, revenue at exit, revenue multiple at exit...the list goes on. What you can do is use a combination of comps, your gut, a unit model, financials, and the team you are backing to better understand the risk/reward profile that sits in front of you, as well as the sensitivity of variables when things go astray or if the company outperforms.

---

[23] To learn more, visit: https://www.amazon.com/Power-Law-Venture-Capital-Making/dp/052555999X

Day 3: **How to conduct Returns Analysis**

Fred Kauber – Stripes

Overview

Many VCs look at returns in two ways:

1. MOIC, or multiple on invested capital. The amount of money an investment returns divided by the amount of money invested

2. IRR, or internal rate of return. The rate of return (or "interest rate") on an investment that you'd have to get to be indifferent between

   a. Keeping the money you'd allocate for the investment

   b. Receiving the future cash flows you'd get from making the investment

Most VCs make investments when they believe that the MOIC or IRR on an investment clears a certain "hurdle" they've defined. While that hurdle can be subjective, VCs know that they need to set realistic and competitive hurdles to raise money from LPs

Basic Example

A basic returns analysis has 3 key inputs:

1. Entry Deal Terms (Pre-Money Valuation + Investment Amount)
2. Subsequent Dilution
3. Exit Multiple

Entry Deal Terms

Here, it's just helpful to know a few simple equations, explained in greater detail here:

$$Post\ Money\ Valuation\ =\ Pre\ Money\ Valuation\ +\ Total\ Primary\ Capital\ Invested\ in\ the\ Round$$

$$Your\ Firm's\ Ownership\ After\ the\ Round\ =\ \frac{Amount\ of\ Capital\ Your\ Firm\ Invested}{Post\ Money\ Valuation}$$

Subsequent Dilution

It's very unlikely that your firm's ownership at the time of an investment will be the same as your firm's ownership when you exit the business. The main reason is dilution, or a reduction in your firm's ownership percentage because of the issuance of new shares. Dilution matters because it impacts your firm's ownership at exit.

$$\%\ Ownership\ at\ Exit\ =\ \%\ Ownership\ at\ Investment\ \ x\ \ (1\ -\ Dilution\ Percentage)$$

Your firm's ownership position could be diluted for many reasons, especially if the company you've invested in decides to:

- Take on additional funding, in which case it will need to issue new shares to the new investors

- Increase the option pool to incentivize existing employees

If you're calculating your firm's returns at the time of exit, then you don't need to worry about forecasting dilution because it has already happened. Your firm's ownership (and portion of the proceeds generated by the sale of the company) will be:

$$\frac{Fully-Diluted\ Shares\ Your\ Firm\ Owns\ at\ Exit}{Total\ Fully-Diluted\ Share\ Count}$$

However, if you're projecting what your firm's return profile will be at exit when you're making the investment, you have to assume how much future dilution there will be. There are rules of thumb you can follow (e.g., if you're expecting your company to be a massive IPO in the future, you can estimate around 40-50% dilution after investing in the Seed round, 30-40% dilution after investing in the A, 20-30% dilution after investing in the B, etc). That said, how much dilution your investment will face depends on several factors, including:

1. Expected exit path for the company: for example, if you expect the company will raise a lot of money over multiple years on a path to IPO, plan for more dilution. However, if you expect the company will exit via acquisition in a few years without raising much more, plan for less dilution

2. Industry the company operates in: for example, if you believe the company operates in a competitive market, plan for more dilution. The company will need to issue more shares/options to attract/retain good talent

3. State of the company's leadership: if the company still needs to hire key leadership positions, plan for more dilution. As above, the company will need to issue more shares/options to attract those leaders

Exit Multiple

Companies often exit (go public via IPO, get acquired, etc) at a multiple of some key metric, called the "exit multiple". Most companies will exit/trade at a multiple comparable to their peer set. For example, many software businesses are valued off a prevailing market multiple of annual recurring revenue ("ARR"). The more similar the peer set of companies, the more accurate the comparable exit multiple.

$$Exit\ Value\ of\ Company\ =\ Exit\ Multiple\ x\ Key\ Operating\ Metric\ That\ Drives\ Multiple$$

Pro-tip: to gather exit multiples, check out what comparable companies are valued at. For example, visit Meritech's Enterprise Comparables[24] page, Pitchbook, or Public Comps[25].

Some companies will exit for a higher multiple than their peers if they

1. Perform better than their peers across a key metric that matters to investors/acquirers (e.g., revenue growth, gross margin, etc)

2. Have strategic value to their acquirer (e.g., Facebook's acquisition of Instagram[26])

Proceeds at Exit

When you invest in a startup, you will generate most/all of your proceeds from an exit event.

---

[24] To learn more, visit: https://www.meritechcapital.com/public-comparables/enterprise#/public-comparables/enterprise/valuation-metrics

[25] To learn more, visit: https://publiccomps.com/

[26] To learn more, visit: https://www.vox.com/2017/4/9/15235940/facebook-instagram-acquisition-anniversary

To see how all these things flow together, including a sample MOIC and IRR table, check out the example here:

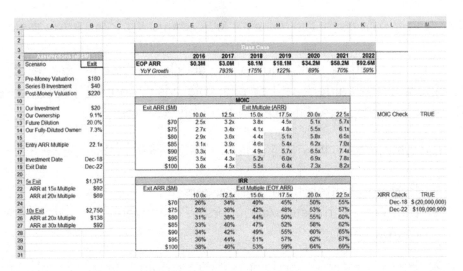

Other Complications

Returns calculations can be a lot more complicated. Modeling out returns can be more difficult when dealing with:

- Complex "preference stacks" (explained more below)

- Dividends, or when an investor is paid out a share of the profits the company generates. This increases an investor's return/IRR on an investment

- SAFE notes with valuation caps and/or discount notes

The standard, or "clean" security, in most private investments is a convertible preferred with a 1x liquidation preference. A few key terms below:

- Preferred: a security type "senior" to common stock, meaning preferred stockholders get paid back before common stockholders

- Pari-Passu: suggests that all shareholders of a given type are of equal seniority. For example, many Series B investors will specify that their Preferred Stock is pari-passu with the Series A investors to ensure they all get paid in equal rates at the same time

- Liquidation Preference: entitles the preferred shareholder to their preference before less senior shareholders are paid (e.g., if it's a 1x preference, we make 1x our money in the event of an exit before anyone else less senior gets paid anything)

- Dividend: a guaranteed annual rate of return on an investment. For example, if my investment in a company specifies an 8% dividend with a 1x liquidation preference, I'm guaranteed to make 1x my money plus ~8% for each year of my investment

- Convertible: holder has the right to convert to common stock (e.g., in the event of an exit like an IPO, a preferred stockholder can convert their stock to common stock and participate in the exit event to generate proceeds)

- Participatory Rights: after a liquidation preference has been executed, Preferred Stockholders get a share of the remaining proceeds equal to their ownership of the company, regardless of whether the Common Stockholders have gotten an amount equal to the liquidation preference first (see example below)

- Cap: a limit on how much of a return an investment can generate

Marcus Gosling[27] gives some great examples of how this all works on a $2M investment to own 50% of a business with a post-money

---

[27] To learn more, visit: https://tools.ltse.com/funding-your-startup-a-founders-guide-to-liquidation-preferences-e7db39469463

valuation of $4M. In this simple example, preferred stockholders own 50%, and common stockholders own 50%

Example 1: No Liquidation Preference - note preferred stockholders and common stockholders get paid together in lockstep

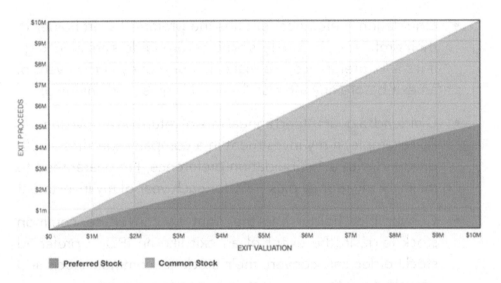

Example 2: 1x Liquidation Preference, Convertible Preferred

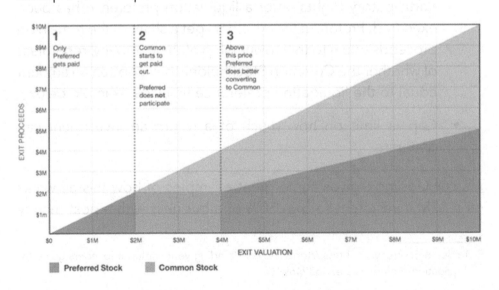

- **Note:** preferred stockholders get paid 1x their $2M investment before common stockholders are paid anything

- Then, preferred stockholders take 50% of all remaining proceeds alongside common stockholders

Example 4: 1x Liquidation Preference, Participating with 2x Cap

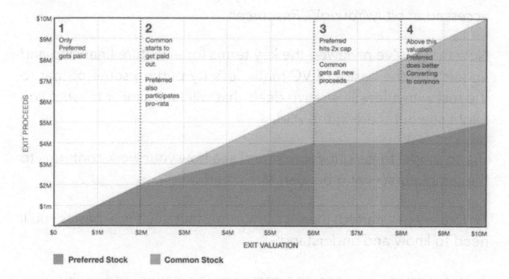

- Here, preferred is limited in their participatory rights up to $4M of proceeds

- Once the common stockholders have also recouped $4M, both the preferred and common stockholders start to participate in the upside 50/50 again

Day 4: **How to present dynamic cap tables**

Yoni Rechtman at Slow Ventures

This chapter includes an accompanying spreadsheet which can be accessed at bit.ly/YoungVCResources

Now that you've reviewed the key terms for a venture financing and understand the basics of VC math, let's try putting some of that to the test with a few illustrative deals that will look similar to what you might see out there in the wild.

Try to model these out yourself and see how your work conforms to the template/scenario builders I've created.

Before we get started, there's a few important, technical basics you'll need to know and understand:

1. In a *primary issuance*, the company is creating and selling new shares to investors. Investors' money goes from their pockets to the company's balance sheet; no existing shares change hands and no existing shareholders realize any profit.
a)Compare this to a *secondary sale* whereby existing investors, founders, employees, etc. sell their shares (common or preferred) to an investor without that money reaching the company's balance sheet. Investors and employees do this to take money out of the company like you might sell some of your shares from your brokerage account.
b)Though they may include some smaller secondary sales, most venture deals will be primary sales as companies create and sell stock to raise money for their own operations. Public markets, on

the other hand, are largely made up of secondary sales as investors trade shares between themselves with the occasional new primary issuance by new (IPOs) or existing public companies.

2. By and large, _each new financing will create a new share class_. So Series A will create Series A Preferred shares, Series B will create Series B Preferred shares, and so on.

a) When SAFEs and convertible notes convert into preferred shares ahead of a Series A round, for example, they will often be labeled as Series Seed-1 Preferred, Series Seed-2 Preferred, and so on. When it comes to shares from SAFEs and notes, the numbers generally go in reverse order such that Seed-4 might be the pre-seed round and Seed-1 will be the round closest to Series A. This is purely a convention of the form and not a requirement but generally speaking, the converted shares will be named based on the financing round they convert into. So the pre-seed SAFEs that convert at the seed will be labeled as Seed-1 while the "seed extension" shares raised between the priced seed round and the priced series A will be labeled as Series A-1 shares.

b) You'll very often be reviewing outputs from Carta where things will be labeled as PS (Seed Preferred)), PA (Series A Preferred), PB (Series B Preferred), PA-1 (Series A-1 Preferred), etc. Ideally Carta would output the shares based on the issuance date or seniority, but it generally does not work that way. Be sure you know for yourself what each share class really really represents. Pro tip! You can always look at the share prices from each round to determine 1) the post-money valuation at that round (assuming not new options were created along the way and 2)

3. When we talk about pre-money and post-money, we don't just mean the valuation. This often literally refers to before and after the

money has come in/before and after the financing is completed. This is especially salient for understanding option pool mechanics.

4. When companies grant shares to employees as part of compensation packages, those shares are awarded in the form of stock options and come out of a designated number of shares reserved for employees known as the *option pool*. As options are allocated to new employees (and awarded as bonuses or in retention plans) the pool is depleted. Moreover, the collective ownership of the total options (both issued and unissued) gets diluted along with the rest of the shareholders as the company issues new shares to raise money from investors. To compensate for that and provide more shares to hire new employees, financing rounds will typically include an *option pool top-off*, whereby the company creates new options to bring the total unallocated pool to some target percentage of the total capitalization upon completion of the financing (the *post-money option pool*).

a)The option pool can be increased and the new options can be issued either pre-money or post-money - before or after the new preferred shares are created and sold to investors, respectively. This has major implications for dilution and ownership. A *pre-money option pool increase* puts all the dilution on the existing shareholders of the company whereas a *post-money option pool increase* also dilutes the investors who just got their shares in the round. As such, the overwhelming majority of term sheets will specify and use language like "a pre-money increase to the option pool to achieve an unallocated post-money post-money option pool of ___%." This spares the new investors from the dilution of the increase and hits the existing shareholders with two rounds of dilution: they get diluted by the new options AND by the new preferred shares.

5. Calculating share prices is simple except when it's not. As a general rule of thumb, you _calculate share price by dividing a valuation by a share count_ (literally price/share).

a)In the case of a priced round, the numerator (price) will be the pre-money valuation. Swapping the new shares for the cash doesn't create value on the balance sheet; it just adds cash and asset and a proportional amount of shareholder equity. The denominator (shares) will be the number of shares immediately prior to the financing - once everything has converted and all the options have been created (assuming a pre-money increase to the option pool).

b)In a post-money YC SAFE (the most common and standardized convertible security), the numerator will simply be the post-money valuation cap. The denominator will be defined in the SAFE as "Company Capitalization, which is the sum of all existing prior to the converting event and - here's the tricky part - that _Company Capitalization includes the shares from the SAFE conversion_.

6. Creating new shares for an option pool or for a SAFE/note conversion where the existing capitalization includes the new shares/options sounds confusing and circular because it is! The only way you can do this math is to _turn on iterative calculations_ (aka "circular references") in XLS/Google Sheets.

Now on to the scenarios!

[QR CODE]

	Pre-financing					Post-Financing					
Name	Common Shares	Options	Seed Pref	FD Shares	FD %	Common Shares	Options	Seed Pref	Seed-1 Pref	FD Shares	FD %
Common Holders											
Co-founder #1	4,000,000			4,000,000	34.78%	4,000,000				4,000,000	31.30%
Co-founder #2	4,000,000			4,000,000	34.78%	4,000,000				4,000,000	31.30%
Option Pool											
Issued		750,000		750,000	6.52%		750,000			750,000	5.87%
Unissued		750,000		750,000	6.52%		750,000			750,000	5.87%
Preferred Holders											
Seed			2,000,000	2,000,000	17.39%			2,000,000		2,000,000	15.65%
Seed-1									1,277,777	1,277,777	10.00%
FD Shares	8,000,000	1,500,000	2,000,000	11,500,000	100.00%	8,000,000	1,500,000	2,000,000	1,277,777	12,777,777	100.00%
FD %	69.57%	13.04%	17.39%	100.00%		62.61%	11.74%	15.65%	10.00%	100.00%	

Seed-1 Round		
Post-money	$25,000,000	<assumption
Round size	$2,500,000	<assumption
Pre-money	$22,500,000	
Pre-money capitalzation	11,500,000	
PPS	$1.96	
Shares	1,277,777	

Scenario #1 - Issuing New Shares

- Pre-financing

  - Two co-founders with 4 million common shares each

  - 1.5 million options, 750,000 of which have been issued to employees

  - 2 million shares held by pre-seed investors

- Seed

  - $2.5 priced round on $25 million post-money valuation

	Pre-financing					Post-Financing						
Name	Common Shares	Options	Seed Pref	FD Shares	FD %	Common Shares	Options	Seed Pref	Series A-1 Pref	Series A Pref	FD Shares	FD %
Common Holders												
Co-founder #1	4,000,000			4,000,000	34.78%	4,000,000					4,000,000	24.73%
Co-founder #2	4,000,000			4,000,000	34.78%	4,000,000					4,000,000	24.73%
Option Pool												
Issued		750,000		750,000	6.52%		750,000				750,000	4.64%
Unissued		750,000		750,000	6.52%		750,000				750,000	4.64%
Preferred Holders												
Seed			2,000,000	2,000,000	17.39%			2,000,000			2,000,000	12.37%
SAFE Investors									1,437,499		1,437,499	8.89%
Series A										3,234,374	3,234,374	20.00%
FD Shares	8,000,000	1,500,000	2,000,000	11,500,000	100.00%	8,000,000	1,500,000	2,000,000	1,437,499	3,234,374	16,171,873	100.00%
FD %	69.57%	13.04%	17.39%	100.00%		49.47%	9.28%	12.37%	8.89%	20.00%	100.00%	

SAFE Financing

Post-money	$25,000,000
Round size	$2,500,000
Implied Pre-money	$22,500,000
Company Capitalization	12,937,499
Implied PPS	$1.74
Shares	1,437,499

Series A

Post-money	$50,000,000
Round size	$10,000,000
Pre-money	$40,000,000
Pre-money capitalization	12,937,499
PPS	$3.09
Shares	3,234,374

Scenario #2 - Converting the SAFE at Series A

- Pre-financing
  - Two co-founders with 4 million common shares each
  - 1.5 million options, 750,000 of which have been issued to employees
  - 2 million shares held by pre-seed investors
  - $2.5 million on $25 million post-money SAFE[28]

---

[28] I am not including a *discount rate* in these models. In brief, a discount rate of say 20% (confusingly this will often expressed instead as 80% or 1 minus the discount rate) stipulates that if the valuation at the next round is lower than the valuation of the SAFE, you'd instead just convert at discount to that round, offering protection against a down-round. Most of the time, you won't have to actually worry about this and when you do you're screwed anyway but good to keep in the back of your head.

- Series A

  o $10 priced round on $50 million post-money valuation

	Pre-financing					Post-Financing						
Name	Common Shares	Options	Seed Pref	FD Shares	FD %	Common Shares	Options	Seed Pref	Series A-1 Pref	Series A Pref	FD Shares	FD %
Common Holders												
Co-founder #1	4,000,000			4,000,000	34.78%	4,000,000					4,000,000	21.81%
Co-founder #2	4,000,000			4,000,000	34.78%	4,000,000					4,000,000	21.81%
Option Pool												
Issued		750,000		750,000	6.52%		750,000				750,000	4.09%
Unissued		750,000		750,000	6.52%		750,000				750,000	4.09%
New Options				0	0.00%		1,542,653				1,542,653	8.41%
Preferred Holders												
Seed			2,000,000	2,000,000	17.39%			2,000,000			2,000,000	10.90%
SAFE Investors				0	0.00%				1,630,331		1,630,331	8.89%
Series A				0	0.00%					3,668,246	3,668,246	20.00%
FD Shares	8,000,000	1,500,000	2,000,000	11,500,000	100.00%	8,000,000	3,042,653	2,000,000	1,630,331	3,668,246	18,341,230	100.00%
FD %	69.57%	13.04%	17.39%	100.00%		43.62%	16.59%	10.90%	8.89%	20.00%	100.00%	

SAFE Financing	
Post-money	$25,000,000
Round size	$2,500,000
Implied Pre-money	$22,500,000
Company Capitalization	14,672,964
Implied PPS	$1.53
Shares	1,630,331

Series A	
Post-money	$50,000,000
Round size	$10,000,000
Pre-money	$40,000,000
Pre-money capitalization	14,672,964
PPS	$2.73
Shares	3,668,246

Scenario #3 - Option pool top-off

- Pre-financing

  o Two co-founders with 4 million common shares each

  o 1.5 million options, 750,000 of which have been issued to employees

  o 2 million shares held by pre-seed investors

  o $2.5 million on $25 million post-money SAFE

- Series A

  o $10 priced round on $50 million post-money valuation

  o Pre-money increase for a 12.5% post-money option pool

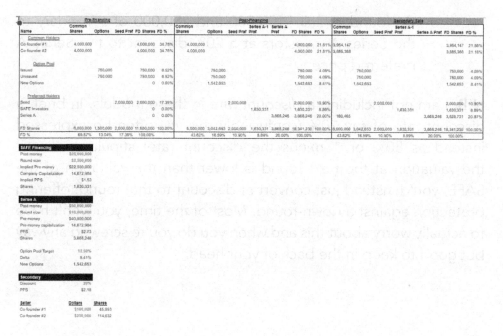

Scenario #4 - Selling secondary

- Pre-financing

  o Two co-founders with 4 million common shares each

  o 1.5 million options, 750,000 of which have been issued to employees

  o 2 million shares held by pre-seed investors

  o $2.5 million on $25 million post-money SAFE

- Series A

    o $10 priced round on $50 million post-money valuation

    o   Pre-money increase for a 10% post-money option pool

    o   Co-founders sell $100,000 and 250,000 of secondary to
        the Series A investors at a 20% discount to the Series A
        preferred price

N.B. I am not including a *discount rate* in these models. In brief, a
discount rate of say 20% (confusingly this will often be expressed
instead as 80% or 1 minus the discount rate) stipulates that if
the valuation at the next round is lower than the valuation of the
SAFE, you'd instead just convert at discount to that round, offering
protection against a down-round. Most of the time, you won't have
to actually worry about this and when you do you're screwed anyway
but good to keep in the back of your head.

Day 5: **Advanced concepts in deal structuring**

Taylor Davidson at Foresight.is

Now that you have learned a bit about financing rounds and understand how the math works to use valuations to calculate share prices, issue shares, and model fundraising rounds from Yoni's piece on cap tables, time to dive into a few topics that can easily be misunderstood.

1. **The difference between issuing promissory instruments vs. actual share issuances:** Many financing rounds do not involve a primary issuance of new shares, at least not right away. SAFEs and convertible notes differ from priced equity rounds in that SAFEs and convertible notes do not yet give the buyers of those instruments ownership of shares, just the right to purchase shares at a time in the future at a price to be determined. Convertible notes and SAFEs are generally converted into equity when an equity round is raised. Shares are purchased with the same rights as the new equity round, but usually for a different price.

2. **Understanding the 'best' time to use a capital raising instrument:** SAFEs, convertible notes, and priced equity rounds are all methods for companies to bring in investment capital, the "right" one to use can vary by the situation.

   a. SAFEs generally use standardized documents, limiting the legal overhead and cost associated with bringing in capital, and are well understood within the early-stage funding community.

b. Equity rounds involve a lot more structure, negotiation, cost, and time to execute, but will be required for larger and later funding rounds.

Each have different default structural components that make sense for different situations; for example, SAFEs are easy to use to bring in investment capital when needed as the company grows at different valuations (prices), providing a lot of flexibility for founders, but that often comes with the cost of extra dilution to founders when the SAFEs convert to equity (the default postmoney SAFEs, for example, effectively provide anti-dilution protection to investors until they convert into equity). SAFEs may make less sense to investors at later stages if there is less guarantee the company will raise future equity rounds, making convertible notes a more effective structure for some financings; notes are often used for early-stage financings, and may make more sense for bridge rounds if there is a risk of anti-dilution provisions being triggered from existing equity shareholders.

The key point is that each legal vehicle offers pros and cons for founders and investors at different stages, and the important thing is to work with transaction principals who have experience with the various options and can help you choose the right one.

3. **Understand the difference between authorized, issued and fully-diluted shares:** There are a few different ways to think of the share count, most importantly authorized, issued, and fully-diluted.

a. Authorized shares are the number of shares that a company is legally allowed to issue by the company's operating and shareholder agreements, and this can be changed by the company's board of directors if needed.

b. Issued shares are the shares that are owned by investors, the sum of all the different share classes mentioned previously, and can include common and preferred shares.

c. Fully-diluted shares includes issued shares (on an as-converted basis, in case any issued preferred shares have the right to convert to different numbers of common shares), and adds shares reserved to issue under options and warrants.

The important thing to remember is that governance and control will often be based on ownership of issued shares, most calculations of share prices will rely on fully-diluted shares, and that authorized shares can be changed if a company needs to issue or reserve more shares.

4. **How to calculate share prices accurately:** Adding to the previous points on share price calculations, you _calculate share price by dividing a valuation by a share count_, with the note that all of the complications around calculating share prices come from the question of what shares are included in that share count. Issuing shares to new equity investors, converting SAFEs to equity, and reserving new shares for option pools and warrants all involve increasing the total number of shares, thus reducing the ownership percentage for all the existing shareholders prior to the round. That dilution (ownership dilution) can vary depending on what shares are included in the share count used to calculate the share prices

(which determine how many shares are issued or reserved for the investment capital received).

5. **Pre-money vs. post-money:** This is the "premoney" and "postmoney" concept, and it's commonly and easily misunderstood; the key thing to remember is that all of the terminology and math is about who bears the dilutive effect of issuing or reserving new shares, and usually it's a question of how the dilution is borne by (a) all shareholders, including new equity shareholders investing in a round, (b) existing shareholders prior to the round, and (c) some mixture of the two. The more shares included in the share count used in the calculation, the more the existing shareholders are being diluted, the lower the valuation that the existing shareholders are effectively getting for the new investment. Each investment instrument has different default methods for calculating share prices, with different implications.

6. **Consider _net_ impact:** It is commonly thought that one method or the other is better or worse for different parties, and while that's true, always remember that you can make the methods equivalent by changing the valuation. Best practice is to negotiate the price of a new investment round at the same time as negotiating how conversions and option pools are being handled, so that people understand the full net impact.

7. **Where to look for guidance:**If you ever get confused by what the terminology means and how to handle different situations, read the legal documents. Shareholder documents (typically the share purchase agreement, or SPA) will typically specify how to calculate share prices in a conversion, specifying exactly how to calculate share prices and share counts, and

commonly vary from the standard agreements as the result of negotiation or adjustment for particular situations.

8. **Accounting for dilution:** Everybody cares about dilution, but it's important to understand the different types of dilution and ways to deal with it. Ownership dilution is when the ownership percentage (the portion of the company a shareholder owns) decreases, usually through the issuance of new shares. Value dilution is when the value of a shareholder's investment goes down, usually through the issuance of new shares at a lower price than shareholders previously paid (a "down round", technically, the issuance of new shares at a premoney valuation less than the postmoney valuation of a previous round).

9. **Not all dilution is created equal:** Ownership dilution can be normal and healthy if the share price is increasing, as the value of the shareholder's investment can go up even if they own a smaller part of the company. To guard against ownership dilution, significant investors will often have rights of first refusal (prorata rights) to give them the opportunity to buy new shares to maintain their ownership percentage (excluding some carveouts like reductions in ownership coming from new shares reserved for options), and less commonly, rights to be issued new shares for free to maintain their ownership portion.

10. **Nuances in anti-dilution provisions:** Value dilution can be more damaging to a company's morale and capitalization table, impacting all shareholders and option holders by reducing the value of their holdings. To guard against value dilution, significant investors will often have anti-dilution protections that either (a) issue them new shares or more commonly, (b) change the ratio at which their existing

preferred shares convert into common shares. These protections can range from full compensation (full ratchet anti-dilution, which maintains the value of their investment) to partial compensation (weighted average anti-dilution). The value of weighted-average protection varies whether the broad-based or narrow-based method of calculation is used, the key difference being a technical distinction on whether the share count used in the formula includes options and warrants (broad-based) or excludes them (narrow-based).

11. **Pro rata rights:** Investors vary on approach, but generally want to have the right to participate in future financing rounds - pro rata rights - so that they can deploy capital into companies that are doing well, even if the valuations are increasing. The common question for investors is "how much do I have to invest to maintain my ownership", and the usual answer is actually pretty easy, being the ownership percentage they had prior to the round times the amount of new capital coming into the round, and to remember that even with pro rata rights, investors can get diluted if new shares are being reserved for options or warrants as part of the round. SAFEs and convertible notes generally don't have pro rata rights for new convertible investments, but it is common for investors and founders to discuss if investors want to participate in new financings made using those vehicles.

Now that you understand how capitalization tables are created and adjusted as companies raise capital, let's cover how they are used when a company sells itself, and how the proceeds are distributed amongst shareholders.

1. **Exit waterfalls** are how people figure out how much in cash and/or shares to distribute to shareholders in a liquidity event

like an acquisition, merger, or initial public offering. Waterfalls are also commonly created as part of financing rounds so that investors and founders can create views of what their returns could look like from the investment round, given different exit scenarios, and thus are commonly created to show what the distribution looks like under a range of exit valuations.

2. **Why it's called a 'waterfall':** The best way to think of modeling a liquidity distribution is that the proceeds from an exit are "flowing" down through the classes of shareholders. The liquidity distribution thus models down through each class of shareholders, from the most senior to the most junior, down to common shareholders and option holders, evaluating each of the rights and terms of their particular investments, to see what they receive, given what other investors do. Remember the goal of the terms around preferred (liquidity preferences, conversion ratio, dividends, etc.) are to shape returns outside of just the exit valuation.

3. **Preferred stock considerations:** Preferred shareholders usually have two important features to their investments:

   a. They have liquidity preferences on the value of their invested capital, meaning they get the right to get their money back before shareholders junior to them.

   b. They can choose to "take their preference" or convert their preferred shares to common shares, and take their share of proceeds alongside common.

4. **When does the preferred stack convert?** Preferred shareholders will choose the option that results in the largest returns for them, given what other investors choose to do. Thus, understanding how to test whether an investor holding

preferred shares takes their liquidation preference or converts their preferred shares to common is the most important part of creating an exit waterfall.

a. This option to "take their preference" is what creates the preference stack at a company, meaning the total amount of proceeds that must be paid to preferred shareholders before common shareholders can share in the distribution.

5. **What if some investor instruments haven't converted before an exit?** If there are SAFEs or convertible notes held by investors that have yet to convert, read the agreements to see how to handle them in a liquidity event in absence of a funding event. Typically SAFEs will convert into shares and be treated as a preferred shareholder, whereas convertible notes have more variability in how they should be treated. This ranges from a simple redefined payout as a multiple of invested capital (which would occur *before* distributions to equity holders), to being converted into preferred shares as some agreed upon terms.

6. **Dissecting 'participating' preferred:** The total amount of liquidation preferences can often be thought of as the total amount of capital invested in the company, but preferred shareholders often have additional terms that can increase their preferences (usually a multiple of their invested capital), allow them to both take their preference and share in the distribution to common (participating preferred, which can be full participating or can have a cap on the total participation), and increase their share of the distribution to common by converting their preferred shares into a larger number of common shares (the conversion ratio). All of these tools provide the potential for increased returns to preferred

shareholders, and are ways for investors and founders to structure investment rounds where founders can get higher valuations at time of investment, in return for greater returns to investors at time of exit. Thus the impact of each should be carefully considered at time of investment.

7. **Where does the common stack sit?** Common shareholders receive whatever is left after preferred shareholders take their liquidity preferences. At valuations higher than the total preference stack, after accounting for the terms of the preferred, preferred shareholders will typically opt to waive their liquidity preferences by converting their preferred shares to common.

8. **Where do option holders (oftentimes employees) fall in the equation?** Option holders also have a choice, whether to exercise their options or not. Options are exercised by buying their options at the strike price so that they can own common stock and receive the distributions per share of common stock.

   a. Options will be "in the money" if the proceeds per share is greater than their strike price, and "out of the money" if the proceeds per share is lower than the strike price.

   b. Options where the strike price is lower than the proceeds per share will not be exercised. The key to options is that exercising options increases the number of common shares used in the calculation of proceeds per share, and also increases the total proceeds, as the amount that option holders pay to exercise the options are typically paid to the company and are added to the amount distributed to shareholders.

- **Tying it all together:** Waterfalls are by nature very circular because the choices that preferred shareholders and option holders make are all interdependent on what other shareholders make. Different shareholders will have invested at different valuations (and thus have different liquidity preferences per share), and different option holders will have different strike prices (and thus have different decisions on whether to exercise at different exit valuations), creating a mesh of interconnected decisions that require circular references and iterative calculation methods for spreadsheets to solve correctly.

For more information and detailed workouts, please visit https:// foresight.is/cap-tables

WEEK 7

WINNING DEALS & BUILDING A REPUTATION

Day 1: **How do you win a deal in a competitive environment - Part I**

Claire Pan – Inspired Capital

Winning the deal is arguably one of the most important skills you can have as an investor because knowing an opportunity is "good" doesn't matter if you ultimately don't have the opportunity to invest.

"Winning the Deal" happens long before a term sheet is actually given

Time management is often the hardest part of being a VC. When you're juggling a handful of exciting deals, urgent portfolio needs, and a wave of internal tasks, work can quickly become overwhelming and it's easy to start treating diligence like a checklist that helps you get to conviction (or not) as quickly as possible. It's important to recognize that every interaction you have with a founder, whether it be in-person or even through text, is a datapoint they are collecting on what it might be like to work with you. You can proactively put yourself in a position to win the deal by impressing them at every step. Being extremely prepared for meetings, asking thoughtful questions, and running a tight process are easy examples of ways that junior VCs can stand out. The last thing any founder wants, for example, is to spend a few weeks and countless meetings with you only for your partnership to ask very basic questions that have already been answered 100 times. I strongly believe that creating a great diligence experience sets the tone of what it would be like to work with you.

Winning the deal is not just about maximizing value for yourself and your firm

One of my favorite books from the Inspired Reading List is *Never Split the Difference*, a guide on negotiations from Chris Voss, the FBI's former lead international kidnapping negotiator. It's obvious that winning deals involves negotiations, but it's not obvious that negotiating has a lot to do with active listening. A surprisingly simple but important takeaway from the book is that winning a negotiation is rarely about trying to get as much as possible from the other person, but more about reaching an outcome that makes both parties happy. You have to understand what's really important to you, and what's really important to the founder, so you can find a way for both of you to win. Giving a term sheet that doesn't align with what is important to the founders is a sign that you don't understand them and will probably only work when there's no other options at the table.

Lean in quickly and trust your instincts

One of easiest way to lose a deal is losing on speed. There are so many incidents where other investors have met the founders first (and sometimes have been in conversation with them for years) and took so long to do their full diligence that another investor had swooped in and taken the deal off the table. Being the first to give a term sheet to a founder is a real vote of confidence – and is hugely relieving for any founder – so moving quickly and decisively is meaningful. Unless you have a special relationship or a particularly unique value add, I find that it becomes infinitely more difficult to win when there are too many other term sheets and you end up competing on price. At Inspired, we're very focused on carving out time for thesis work throughout the year because we believe that doing the research beforehand makes it much easier for us to recognize when something is special and aligns with how we see the world evolving. It also gives us the confidence to move quickly without having to do a bunch of Googling on the market or scramble to find experts in our network that can share their feedback with us.

Have an arsenal of resources specifically for winning the deal

Winning the deal is often time-sensitive. One of the ways to proactively prepare is by having a library of compelling options you can leverage so you don't have to reinvent the wheel every time. At Inspired, we like to introduce companies to our existing founders so they can get a true sense of what it's like to work with us. This is especially helpful when we've invested in another company in a similar category or has a similar business model. At the same time, we also like to find time to share all the ways we support our founders because every company has different priorities. We know that "platform" also means very different things across firms so we find it helpful to be explicit about what it means for us. The exact playbook should be customized each time, but it helps when you go into a process knowing exactly what you can offer.

Know the ways that you as an individual can help win a deal

The above four points largely focus on ways that a fund can win a deal, but I also wanted to touch on a few ways that individuals can position themselves for success. The first is to know your value-add. For me, my background in growth investing and helping companies fundraise might be attractive to founders who want hands-on help with building financial models, thinking through unit economics, and creating the right data room. The second is to show your value-add. If you're selling on the point that you can make helpful customer introductions, you might give a list of people at specific companies that you are well-connected with or, even better, proactively make a couple of introductions. The last is to think deeply about your network. While you might not be best friends with famous investors or CEOs, everyone's network is unique, and you probably know someone who can be helpful to the company.

Overall, the way that I think about honing this skill is by learning from investors I deeply respect and imitating them while adding my own personal style over time.

Day 2: **How do you win a deal in a competitive environment - Part II**

JC Bahr-de Stefano

In today's startup ecosystem, capital for early-stage companies has become commoditized due to the sheer amount of venture capital available. This means that great founders building great companies don't always have trouble raising money. In fact, founders with impressive backgrounds, such as those with prior exits or experience working at successful companies, often find themselves in a position where venture capital funds compete to invest in their companies.

As an early stage venture capitalist, my fund focuses on the quality of the team being invested in. Since many early-stage companies pivot as they iterate and test out their idea with customers, the business that you invest in doesn't always remain the same - what does, is the founding team.

Various methods can convince a founder to take one fund's money over someone else's and, ultimately, different things will resonate with different founders. Here are some of the things that my fund has done in these types of situations in the past:

- **Offer founder references**
    - o During my fund's diligence process, we often perform reference checks on the founding team - this could be with former bosses, colleagues, etc. so that we can get a sense of the founder (strengths and weaknesses, etc.). An investment is a long term partnership so you want

to know as much as you can about a team that you will work with and support for years to come. However, we offer founders the opportunity to do the same on us as a fund - founders should be able to speak with founders you have invested in to get real intel on what the relationship has been like and how you were actually able to help. You should connect founders with not only the "highest flying" founders in your portfolio who will obviously say nice things but also those that you supported when things didn't go as well. Ideally, the founders of your portfolio will sell you to those that you are hoping to invest in.

- **Display the value of your network**

  o The value of many venture capital funds is their network, which spans potential customers, strategic partners, other founders or operators who can give insight and advice, follow on investors, and more. For this, you don't need to wait until you have invested - in fact, you should try to prove your value up front so that founders get a sense of how you operate and the value that you can provide. The best funds *earn* their spot on the cap table.

- **Demonstrate domain expertise**

  o Similar to displaying the value of your network, you should demonstrate what your team brings to the table. Everyone on the investment team at my fund, which focuses on fintech, has experience founding and working at fintech companies. This allows us to provide hands-on support to founders as they think through early stage considerations such as GTM motions, critical partnerships, and competitive positioning, among others. There is no doubt that founders see value in working with investors who have done it before themselves, can empathize with their journey, and help them avoid pitfalls or mistakes that they themselves made. In the past, we have hosted semi-working sessions on product roadmap and strategy with potential founders, which we have found they greatly appreciate.

- **Don't forget the bigger picture**

  o While it is good to be competitive and battle to win the best deals, given the nature of this ecosystem, it is important to remain collaborative and embrace kindness and humility. Winning a deal is never a zero sum game - you want to make sure you are doing right by the company which means that offering to co-lead, offering to step back a bit when you know there is an equally capable counterpart in the ring as well, and understanding that other VCs, as much as they are your competitors in the moment, are really your peers when you take the longitudinal view.

Although the tactics listed above are generally relevant in most circumstances, it is really important to ask founders what they are looking for from a partnership with a VC early on and listen carefully. Every founding team has a unique set of skills and will look for specific things from their investors. It's important to tailor support as needed rather than adopting a one-size-fits-all approach.

Day 3: **How to be a thought partner to founders**

Grahme Taylor - Niya Partners

- Capital is abundant; access often depends on founders liking your firm more on the margin, and you can personally make a difference. VC is a relationship business, and not purely transactional.

- A good relationship with the associate can keep founders warm if GPs aren't immediately available, and if you're tactful, some might be willing to tell you things they won't reveal to a GP. Focus on keeping founders comfortable and engaged.

- To me, value trumps volume on founder conversations

  o For founders where you think the opportunity won't be a fit, be courteous of their time and just don't have the initial conversation (or don't have the next one if you discover it isn't a fit after the first). Don't bother trying to win the deal, if the deal's not going to happen.

    - Politely decline with a couple reasons why, or things that if changed — would make more sense for a chat. Avoid BS'ing them — give *real* reasons that are valuable. If you see issues with their strategy or model, say that in a non-arrogant way.

    - Or, if the company is outside your firm's wheelhouse / your knowledge base, make sure you acknowledge that as the issue — and re-assure them that it isn't a knock on their business. Consider introducing them to someone who knows the space more, and can give you feedback while also providing them with worthwhile advice. Of course, don't hesitate to learn about new spaces if you think there's potential to invest there... learning is one of the best parts of this job, and founders can teach you a lot.

- Founders talk with each other more than ever, and you never know when someone will pivot later and come back to you — or refer another deal — because they respected your honesty.

- You should generally take conversations if they're pre-screened warm intros... as declining these can seem rude.

o For those you *do* think are great prospects, be willing to give yourself time to build a rapport, and focus on being thoughtful.

- I rarely get value from 15 - 20 minute strategy conversations — targeting 30 minutes to an hour is better, depending on who you're dealing with.

- Scheduling back-to-back meeting can also hurt your value-add. Take a few minutes before a meeting to review the deck/materials again, and a few minutes after to collect your thoughts & context switch. Have an idea or two in the back of your mind before you start each chat. A surprising number of VCs come into conversations distracted and ill-prepared.

- Give founders time to speak, and practice active listening. Don't interrupt / cut them off unless absolutely necessary, and show you heard them by summarizing what they said in a few words, before diving into questions. Find the natural pauses in their pitch, or let them get through their story before drilling down (take notes along the way on topics you want to bring up).

- Avoid peppering them with lots of questions or obvious things that were answered in the deck. Focus on asking a handful of the best questions you can come up with, that can evolve into a strategic conversation.

- Don't be afraid of the occasional pause to process / collect your thoughts. This becomes easier when you give yourself enough time for the conversation

- Open-ended questions can often produce more authentic responses, and give you a window into how the founder thinks about the world & their business.

- Don't act like you know more than you do. If you don't understand something, ask for clarification. If you're answering a question based on a small sample size of personal data / experience, make sure you acknowledge that. There's often a stereotype around VC associates that we're arrogant know-it-alls... being authentic and humble can take you far — trying to prove you're smart is usually a turn-off.

- Unless they specifically ask for it and you're qualified to answer, avoid giving prescriptive operational advice. Focus on high-level strategy insights.

- Founders love when you can share data they don't have access to on market dynamics, competitors, metrics & benchmarks that investors look for, or the VC funding landscape in general. Of course, be ethical and don't share information on competitors you've talked with… that founders would be upset if you shared about *their* company.

- Focus on offering a couple memorable insights that exceed the obvious. Strategy conversations can get really fun around customer profiles + ROIs, accelerating moats & positive feedback loops in the business model, taking a long-term view towards scale, and industry dynamics + incentive structures.

- Give founders the space to tell you what *they're* wondering about, and don't try to force the conversation just towards what you want to discuss.

- Offer resources that go beyond your own expertise. Great books/podcasts/articles, research reports, and intros to people who deeply understand the founder's space can be helpful.

- If you're too overloaded to have a conversation with the founder right now, set expectations appropriately and don't ghost them. Tell them that you want to make sure you have the bandwidth for a good conversation, and might need a week or two before it can happen.

o Don't just focus on new investment opportunities, but also keep things warm with portfolio company founders. Access to competitive follow-ons is important.

- Even if you aren't a board member or observer, try to get on a close enough basis with a handful of your portfolio founders where you're comfortable texting each other and spending time socially.

- Share relevant info or insights on their space when you come across it (maybe every month or two), and ask the occasional targeted / thoughtful question. Avoid making founders feel like you're grilling them or overly fixated on their company, but show you're engaged and thinking about them after the investment is made.

- Invite founders to events where they can make valuable connections, and always be thinking about customer and investor intros as appropriate.

- Ask about, and remember, details about their personal lives as appropriate. Make sure they know you care about them as a person, not just as a founder. It's not only intrinsically rewarding, but will also keep them coming back for more advice, and result in more intros to other good founders.

Day 4: **How to create a stellar founder experience**

Taylor Brandt - Headline

Giving a personal touch:

- Often the benefit of junior investors is twofold:

  o 1) many times, you may be closer in age to the founder and can find ways to relate to them, whether it's friends, interests etc.

  o 2) you will likely intimidate them less than your senior partners and allow them to be more open and build a deeper personal relationship.

Prepping the Partner and the founder:

- Before you have a company you would like to introduce to your partners, *PREP THEM BOTH.*

  o Often there may be a personality difference between you and your partner, so make sure the founder isn't off put by this and well equipped to come into the meeting. (e.g. my partner has been at the firm 20+ years, he's had winning investments in these spaces, he loves to surf but he's slightly hard to read)

    - I personally add areas where the founder might be dissuaded by a partner to make sure they are prepared and not offput and highlight the partners strengths so they can focus on those

- You should make sure the founders know who they are going in the room with and what you think will "sell" the partner the most in the business. (e.g. my partner is highly focused on data and product market fit, so can you please spend a good amount of time on these slides)

- You should send the partner prep material ahead of the call and ideally have them discuss the business with your partners and use this information as a refresher

Keeping them updated on your process and dd work as it's happening:

- Oftentimes, the most stressful part of a fundraising process for a founder is trying to time the round correctly and having little to no visibility into where different funds are in their processes.

- To remain top of mind for the founder, continue to update them through your process. Ideally, if it feels appropriate, get their cell phone number and text them. For example, if you have 3-4 days of customer calls, let them know, "I've had some great calls, working through a few more and will ping you on X day," this goes a long way.

Prepping the founders for IC:

- Prep the founders on who will be in attendance

  o I like to send a list and relevant investments and interests that may relate to the team

- Prep the founders on which areas you want them to spend additional time focusing on during the IC to prepare talking points and materials based on your teams hesitations (e.g. can you please spend additional time on GTM efforts and how long it takes for sales reps to ramp)

- Prep the founders on how you want to use the time best

  o I like to allow for 10 minutes for intros on both sides, 40 minutes for pitching and any topics you've asked them to dive into, 10 minutes for final questions

Creating a great experience at IC for the founder:

- Often an IC can feel like an interrogation room of unnamed faces, do what you can to make it a warm and comfortable experience for the founder

- Introduce your whole team

- Allow the team to do a few things to show they are interested → this could be through personal anecdote, showing them how they use the product etc

- Preparing the team with a few questions

Winning the founders over

- Call them after the IC → If your team is leaning positively following your debrief, keep the founders in the loop as you want to make sure they know where your head is at

- Selling the firm: Either on the follow up call or in person, sell the firm and why you think they would be a perfect fit for the founder. Whether this is domain expertise, future capital that you can deploy, brand or platform teams

- Send them a thank you → after the IC, I like to send them a thank you note, maybe with a little piece of gratitude like a Starbucks gift card

- Sell the personal relationship

- If you can get to them in person, do it and give them a good experience (and focus it on their interests)

When it gets competitive:

- Have a portfolio company call them

- Offer founder references

- Find an extra way to win them over (a friend once got a founder a birthday cake... and paid the right price, terms do matter)

Alternative outcome, passing on people you have spent a great deal of time with them:

- **Pick up the phone**

- We can't do this all the time, but if you have used a lot of the founders' time, this is super important. Explain what part of the diligence process couldn't get you or the team across the edge and based on your fund stage, assess how to conclude the conversation.

- If done correctly, and if given real feedback, often they will come back and intro you to their friends

Day 5: **Maintaining a differentiated reputation**

Annia Mirza - Olima Ventures

Part of creating a stellar founder experience is maintaining a differentiated reputation. Regardless of the vertical, stage or geography you've crafted your thesis around, there are (hopefully) going to be times when the deal you want allocation in is fiercely competitive. With investors lining up to throw cheques at these founders left, right and center, it can be difficult for them to know which investor is the right fit for them in the long run after the round is closed and the slew of press releases, tweets and TechCrunch articles have been published.

In these situations, differentiating yourself from other investors is important. Strategies on how to do this will vary between individuals and funds, but I personally have two guiding principles: (1) go beyond help that will probably be offered by most people, like introductions to other investors (this doesn't mean don't do this; it means do this and more!); (2) act like this is your portfolio company before it is.

Whenever I've taken this approach, it's led to some pretty fun situations.

In my first week in VC, we were speaking to a company that was dealing with an interesting problem. They were an early-stage health-tech company based in the US whose customer base was made up mostly of local and international governments. The sizes of these contracts were big for a company of that stage; in total, they were doing around $3M in sales. On paper, this sounds great — but governments generally only pay out their contracts on a net basis after they've been invoiced, and this is assuming the government is a relatively developed one with stable structures and systems that work. This company was also working with governments in less developed countries whose infrastructure definitely did not fall into this category, meaning their timeline for payment was unreliable and not at all tied to the timeline they promised.

At the same time, this company had little cash in the bank. They were running out of runway to make payroll and keep the company operating long enough for their contract revenue to roll in. Their safety net could only keep them afloat for the next couple of months and they were, with increasing urgency, looking for a short-term infusion of cash to fill the gap beyond that. By the time I'd spoken with him, the founder had already tried alternative financing solutions based on future revenue, like Pipe, but was repeatedly turned away. He was told Pipe required a higher volume of lower value customers, whereas he had the opposite — a smaller volume of very high value customers (we're talking in the six figures).

Safe to say, the founder was frustrated and nearing the end of his tether. So I offered to help. For the next week or so, I spent longer than I care to admit on the phone sourcing and speaking with various invoice factoring companies and investors to figure out ways forward. The week took a few weird turns — at one point, we were introduced to whatever the venture equivalent of a loan shark is; we had calls with the kinds of people you would expect in murkier industries with blurrier values, who were asking us to sign off on outrageous terms in exchange for their help. These calls were simultaneously entertaining and very unsettling. (The type where you're looking at each other through Zoom, trying to make eye contact to confirm that this is, indeed, reality). Fortunately, a much better solution presented itself and we didn't have to go down that route, but even having these conversations showed the founder that we cared enough to jump into the trenches with him and figure out a solution together.

In another example, a New York-based company had recently gone remote and was locked into a five-year lease of an office in a prime location in Flatiron. They were burning $120K a month and were looking for ways to recoup the cost. We spent half a day putting together a quick proposal on turning their office into a coworking space for other startups, complete with a pricing analysis of competitor spaces and a list of people who needed office space and the number of desks they needed (the result of a morning spent spamming all of our friends in tech). The company loved the proposal and ended up hiring a community manager to execute on it, who we work closely with now.

These two examples are admittedly on the extreme side — you don't have to go this far or spend this much time on every company (please don't). Other, equally valuable ways to help might be helping a company find their next hire, connecting them to a potential customer or channel partnership opportunity, or just listing out relevant people you know that they can tap into as and when they need it. If you're doing due diligence on a company, chances are that you already have or are in a position to ask for their last investor update. Look through the asks section and see if there's anything there that you can help with. You won't always win the deal, but you'll develop a reputation as someone who genuinely cares about the people they want to invest in, and as a result the founders you speak with will start referring their friends to you regardless of whether they end up becoming your portfolio company or not.

And, on the plus side, putting the reps in to find creative ways to help companies when they need it is good practice for supporting your portfolio.

[A quick posthumous note that there's a difference between differentiating yourself in a good way, and differentiating yourself in a bad way. Don't be the kind of investor that tries to preemptively wire money to founders before they've made a decision, gatekeeps help until founders have signed a term sheet with them, or trash talks other funds and investors — all real-life examples I've heard.]

WEEK 8

PORTFOLIO SUPPORT

Day 1: **What are the basic blocks of portfolio support?**

Joseph Lissak - Olive Tree Capital

Venture investors can support their portfolio companies in a multitude of ways, such as making BD and customer introductions, helping with hiring, fundraising and strategic planning, joining the Board of Directors, and more. Some firms even have dedicated teams to support their portfolio, often referred to as a "platform."

It is crucial for investors to begin every relationship with their portfolio companies by establishing a clear and open line of communication as early as possible – well before the investment is actually made. Starting early gives both sides the opportunity to establish a trusting relationship, and makes the transition from the investment process to the ongoing portfolio support phase much more natural – and if (likely when) the portfolio company needs some guidance, the founder(s) will feel a lot more comfortable asking for it. One way to do this is to share the investment rationale, as well as areas of concern, so that the founders understand how their investor thinks about the business on a deeper level.

It can also be a powerful strategy to begin offering support *before* the investment is finalized – demonstrating the ability to deliver on the value-add promise will kick the relationship off with a "win" and can even help secure (or increase) an allocation in the round. Early wins help increase trust between investors and companies, and jumpstart momentum moving forward.

Once the docs have been signed and the investment has been finalized, it can be productive for the investor to have a quick sync-up with the founding/executive team to dive further into which areas the firm can be most helpful (if this hasn't already been communicated) and how the company wants to receive support. Moving forward from there, it can also be valuable to establish periodic (i.e quarterly) check-in in order to maintain the relationship and momentum.

While it is imperative for investors to make clear the value they can add beyond their capital, it is perhaps equally important to not be overbearing. Most founders/executives (most people, really) strongly dislike being micromanaged – investors should make it clear that they are there to support the company when and how they want it but won't force anything on them. Some teams will ask for ongoing, hands-on support while others may not ask for any support at all. No matter an investor's level of expertise in a certain industry or vertical, the founders will always be the true experts in their own business.

Those who position themselves as true value-add investors will have a better chance of winning the most competitive deals and will likely generate more robust deal flow due to a stronger reputation within the startup community. It also goes without saying that investors who offer real value beyond capital can have a tangible impact on the success of their portfolio companies. While it's best to start early and maintain an open line of communication in order to stay aligned, it's also never too late.

Day 2: **What should you expect in board meetings?**

Desmond Fleming - FirstMark Capital

When I started my career in startups, I had no idea what went on in Board Meetings. It was a massive black box where you knew it was important, and could have an impact on your job, but visibility was limited. Part of being a great VC is being a great board member, and being a great board member is a skill that has to be learned. You start this journey by being a board observer.

My viewpoint is that your role as a board member is two-pronged, on one end you are there to contribute where you can and in a differentiated way relative to the rest of the board, and on the other end - you are there to learn. Every firm is different, but more likely than not if you are talking more than your Partner is during a board meeting, something has gone wrong. Board Meetings are incredible learning opportunities that have real world impacts, here's how I think about how to be an effective board observer:

Pre-Board Meeting

This is a cliche but as Benjamin Franklin's famous quote goes, "If you fail to prepare, you prepare to fail." That adage is 100% applicable to Board Meetings. If you don't take the time to prepare for a Board Meeting, you are more than likely taking up space and wasting the opportunity presented to you.

Finding the time to prepare for board meetings can be incredibly challenging, especially early on in your career as a VC but it will pay dividends. Before attending a board meeting, consider pulling together a "Pre-Board Meeting Packet." The substance of the packet will change depending on the type of business it is, but generally the goal of the packet is for it to serve as a forcing function for you to think critically about the health of the business, its opportunities, and the challenges ahead. Some information that may be relevant in that packet could be comparing plan versus actuals with respect to core KPIs, or identifying which metrics in the business are deteriorating and developing a perspective on why.

Board Meeting

During a board meeting, as I mentioned before your role is two-pronged, you want to add differentiated value relative to other participants and you are there to learn. Because of this dynamic, for the most part in board meetings, you will be listening, taking notes, and ensuring action items are followed up on.

Your goal should be to actively listen and use your judgment on where and when to chime in. This is where the pre-work from the packet comes in handy. Let's say you noticed that SDR productivity has been declining quarter over quarter, but the business is making an argument to invest in increasing the headcount of that team. Provided that other board members are not picking up on the potential misallocation of resources, you should absolutely view it as your responsibility to speak up. Now let's be honest here. Speaking up in a board meeting, particularly for the first time can be intimidating. There's a lot that you don't know, there's context you may not have, and you don't want to look stupid. All that being said, the best thing to do is to get in the habit of speaking up sooner rather than later. The reps and the confidence you gain from it will compound.

Post-Board Meeting

Following board meetings, what I have found to be most helpful is to briefly and in real time ask for feedback. This will give you an opportunity to course correct any action you take as well as get a better sense of the exact support your Partner is looking for during board meetings. The period after a board meeting is also the best time to review your notes while the conversation is still fresh. Linking your post-board meeting review to your next pre-board meeting packet, can be incredibly helpful. A major part of being a productive board observer is to be the person who has a strong command of the details and nuance of the business, and there is no shortcut to developing that expertise.

Day 3: **How to manage a portco fundraise end to end**

Maliekah Harjani - Early-stage Investor and Advisor

Welcome to one of the most crucial topics in this guide – Fundraising. You heard me – helping portfolio companies raise, is literally the most vital contribution to the business model of a VC fund. Subsequent fundraising = higher valuations = MOIC. As an associate in a VC firm, a large part of your portfolio value add is to ensure that companies have access to downstream capital.

I want to start by saying, really, there is no right formula. Some rounds can take place spontaneously because of an outburst of investor inbounds, some may take a little more introductions and pitches. It can depend on several things – investment climate, how similar companies have grown in other markets, founder profiles, and more.

With that in mind, I wanted to share a framework that you could use to help you navigate your companies when it's time to fundraise.

Some items may not be in chronological order, as each fundraising will be different - light touch vs. heavy. In my scenario, I'm going to assume I must "hand-hold" a portfolio founder for their upcoming round. You can use this framework as a checklist - to ensure that the company is bulletproof when they're ready to go to market.

To start, here are some initial questions to ask your founder:

How much runway do you have left? Ideally, you do not want to leave fundraising to the last minute. My rule of thumb is to ensure that there is still 10-18 months of runway before you kick off a fundraise.

What's the target close date? The timeline of a fundraise, depending on size, complexity of data, and investment due diligence mandate of potential investors, can vary. A founder may want to tell their potential lead investor that they are looking to close in the next 1-2 months. Leave some extra time in case of delays in diligence, round negotiations and drafting legal documents. I would say prepare for 2-8 months from first investor chats to final closing.

Constructing a round

I usually use a bottom-up approach to determine the round size and valuation. Instead of shooting out figures, you want to show investors that you're thinking more strategically instead of optimizing for valuation.

I highly recommend reminding founders to demonstrate that raising money is not the main objective of the business.

What I recommend, is to model out the key milestones your portfolio company would like to get to. You may even simplify it – say the goal is to grow 30% average month-on-month in 2022, and 20% average month-on-month in 2023, which will take the company to US$20M in monthly revenue by June 2023. How much cash would the company need to achieve those goals? What's the monthly burn? Ideally you want to raise for 18-24 months runway.

With that key milestone in mind, you are demonstrating that you are choosing the raise amount with a goal in mind. A founder can then pick the dilution they are most comfortable with. Assume it takes US$20M to get to a particular milestone, you can then apply a 20% dilution, which brings you to US$100M post-money valuation or US$80M pre-money valuation.

In some cases, I've seen founders set the valuation, but in many cases, the lead investor helps construct the round and the terms. Either way, a founder must have a sense of the dilution they are comfortable with. In case the round exceeds the level of dilution a founder is willing to take, the lead investor may suggest issuing ESOP and MSOP with the round as well.

Creating a Pitch Deck

I always make sure that I roughly understand what the round is going to look like before I start creating the pitch deck. The entire story of the deck will be presented towards the key milestones and fundraise, so the story must have consistency from the beginning.

Some associates help founders create the pitch deck from scratch, others will just have to review and help prepare for the pitch.

Here's a pitch deck guide:

- **Company purpose Start here:** define your company in a single declarative sentence. This is harder than it looks. It's easy to get caught up listing features instead of communicating your mission.

- **Problem** Describe the pain of your customer. How is this addressed today and what are the shortcomings to current solutions.

- **Solution** Explain your eureka moment. Why is your value prop unique and compelling? Why will it endure? And where does it go from here?

- **Why now?** The best companies almost always have a clear why now? Nature hates a vacuum—so why hasn't your solution been built before now?

- **Market potential** Identify your customer and your market. Some of the best companies invent their own markets.

- **Competition / alternatives** Who are your direct and indirect competitors. Show that you have a plan to win.

- **Business model** How do you intend to thrive?

- **Team** Tell the story of your founders and key team members.

- **Financials** If you have any, please include.

- **Vision** If all goes well, what will you have built in five years?

Source: Sequoia's Business Plan Template

After the deck is ready, plenty of time will be going towards preparing the founders with the pitch – to ensure that it's refined with flow and ease of understanding. You want to throw in some unprecedented practice questions. Most of all, you want to make sure your founders build passion into their pitch.

Building a Data Room

Ideally, you want to create the pitch deck and data room around the same time. If investor chats go well, then they may immediately request a data room so they could share initial analysis with their team or investment committee.

Here's a list of data room items:

1. **Operational metrics:** month-on-month

2. **Profit & Loss statement:** month-on-month

3. **Cap table:** demonstrating cash invested and share allocation

4. **Term sheet (if available):** including all relevant terms

5. **Personal references:** names and contact information of 2 professional references for each of the Founders

6. **Forecast financials:** month-on-month for at least the next 24 months

7. **Org. chart:** including a breakdown of headcount

8. **C-Suite remuneration:** monthly remuneration

9. **Board composition:** including names, companies and Director type

10. Legal documents associated with the **prior fundraising rounds**

11. Proof of **company incorporation**

A data room bonus is to treat it like another tool to story-tell. I suggest that founders do some relevant calculations for the investor, to leave less room for error, but also to use this as an opportunity to show how you plan on tackling current challenges. For example, a company with poor unit economics can present a table on their current economics and demonstrate what their unit economics will look like 2 years from now. The founder can also add notes to describe how they will achieve that UE forecast. For most business models, relevant calculations include UE, CaC/LTV and so forth. This helps show the potential investor that the founder acknowledges the current challenges and have a well-thought-out plan to improve their figures.

Choosing the Right Investor

It's so imperative for us, as associates, to really understand the dynamics of the VC ecosystem we're in. We would have to map out all potential investors, plus understand a) ticket sizes b) fund sizes and downstream capital access c) value-add services d) unique offerings e) vertical focus g) any competing companies in their existing portfolio.

It's crucial to understand the investment criteria for each VC, to help pre-qualify them and maximize time.

Bonus point: if the potential lead has invested in a similar model in another market, that is lucrative and scaled to over US$1B in valuation. This investor would have likely seen some of the early-stage challenges, and the key success drivers. They could bring powerful insights to the table.

Typically, when I map out all the relevant investors, I create a collaborative google-sheet to help manage the process.

Here's a template of a VC Investor Relationship Manager (RM):

Fund	PIC	Tier	Ticket Size?	Potential Lead?	Connection From:	Status	Global Comps in Portco?	Conflicting Portco?	Action from Founders	Action From VC Associate
XX Ventures	Ashley	1	US$10-15M	Y	Malikah / VC Associate	Due Diligence / IC	Y - Unicorn	N	Share dataroom	Back-channel for feedback
XX Ventures		1		N	Founder	Due Diligence	Y - Soonicorn	N		
XX Ventures		1				Pass				Ask for feedback
XX Ventures		1		Y		Due Diligence	N	N		
XX Ventures		1		N		Awaiting Intro	Y - Seed stage	N		
XX Ventures		1		Y		Awaiting Intro				
XX Ventures		1		N		Due Diligence				
XX Ventures	Michael	2		Y		Awaiting Intro				
XX Ventures		2		N		Awaiting Intro				
XX Ventures		2		Y		Pass				
XX Ventures		2		N		First Meeting				
XX Ventures		2		Y		Awaiting Intro				
XX Ventures		2		N		First Meeting				
XX Ventures		2		N		First Meeting				
XX Ventures	Jane	3		N		Due Diligence				
XX Ventures		3		N		Awaiting Intro				
XX Ventures		3		N		Awaiting Intro				
XX Ventures		3		N		First Meeting				
XX Ventures		3		N		First Meeting				

The template above helps me tier the investors into different buckets, to ensure that I'm prioritizing the investors that would be the best fit for the company.

Typically, I always suggest that the first shot at pitches on Week 1 should be with Tier 3 investors. The best feedback comes from other investors, so practice with them until the pitch feels organic before talking to the top 5-10 investors you've strategically selected as Tier 1 investors.

Start Making introductions!

In tech and VC, relationship building is crucial. Whether your portfolio companies are raising or not, you should be building connections from yesterday. The venture community is extremely small – never burn bridges with any investor!

It's also important to know the culture of each VC internally. Some VCs may have associates push for deals, with others, it may have to come directly from the partner. Each VC will have different internal dynamics, so always choose the right PIC. If it does happen to be someone at partner level, feel free to reach out to your partners or other colleagues to make the introduction. I always say that fundraising is and always will be a team effort, so definitely be open to asking for help!

Supporting Due Diligence

I do not have a formula for this, as each investor conducts due diligence in a different way. Some may prefer to set up follow on calls, some may send a list of 100+ questions on an excel sheet.

The only thing I suggest is to be on standby for your founder in case he/she needs help with certain due diligence questions.

Some potential investors may reach out to you directly, as you have an internal view on how the company has evolved, how the space has evolved, existing challenges and bottlenecks, feedback on working with the founders, etc. It's important to be prepared.

One area that you could probably be the most helpful with is back-channelling to get due diligence feedback. Typically, when I know an associate doing due diligence for one of my portfolio companies, I make time to call them and understand their areas of concern if there are any.

During this time, you want to show investors that you have confidence in the company, but also address their concerns. If there are some parts of the business that haven't been figured out yet, that's okay! No start-up is a finished product but ensure that you can pre-empt some challenges and have a plan to address it.

Navigating the First Offer

We won't spend too much time on the nuances of a term sheet since it's already been covered in the previous sections. However, if you've supported your founder closely during their fundraising journey, you may be the first to hear about the term sheet or verbal offer.

The first offer may be the most exciting, but it might not be the right one. Spend time understanding the pros and cons of the offer.

In some cases, the lead investor may have an idea of the round construct and composition (i.e., investors they would like to work with). Perhaps they may be keen to take the entire round, minus the pro-rata amounts from existing investors. In other cases, the founder would have to reach out to other investors as co-lead or follow-on investors.

Ultimately, it's the founder's decision - our role as associates is to be an objective sounding board throughout this process.

Day 4: **How to utilize platforms for success**

Grant Miller - Crossbeam Venture Partners

In the ever-evolving world of venture capital, Young VC's often find themselves in a competitive race to establish themselves and leave a mark. As the industry continues to mature, it can be easy to think that success is simply about spotting the next big startup. For a young VC eager to make a name and grow their career, an appreciation of the various functions that help companies post investment such as platform support can be a game changer, leading to better outcomes for themselves, their firms, and their portfolio companies.

Differentiating in a Crowded Market

In a world flooded with VC's, differentiating oneself is of paramount importance. While traditional due diligence and networking are key components of the job, platform support provides additional value to portfolio companies beyond just capital. By offering resources, mentorship, connections, and operational assistance, a young VC can stand out from the crowd and demonstrate a deeper commitment to the success of the entrepreneur. For example, a VC that can recommend and connect strong engineering candidates to their startups will earn themself and their firm credibility among the VC community. While other VC's get branded as capital allocators, founders will see you and your firm as an integral factor to growing their team, finding customers, and generally someone they want on their team. Founders talk to other founders and talent talks to other talent, the result being a value-add reputation that will lead to deal flow and allocation in competitive rounds.

Building Stronger Relationships

Platform support fosters a more symbiotic relationship between the VC and the startups they back. This isn't a transactional relationship based merely on capital; it becomes a partnership. Entrepreneurs are more likely to trust and rely on VCs who offer platform support, leading to better communication, transparency, and alignment of objectives. As an example, consider helping a founder reformat their board meeting deck and agenda. Providing a template with key reporting indicators for your founders can result in stronger alignment on what is important to the business. Receiving more applicable information means happier internal stakeholders at your firm and happier founders due to reduced communication issues. A Young VC willing to overlook their own ego and build reporting tools to increase transparency between the platform and founders will impress all parties involved.

Enhancing Investment Outcomes

When startups succeed, VCs succeed. By offering platform support, VCs are not just betting on a company but actively contributing to its growth. When underwriting a new investment, great firms not only assess how good the opportunity ahead of them is, but also how they can enhance their growth trajectory. Assisting with talent acquisition, forging strategic partnerships, or providing industry insights can dramatically increase the likelihood of a startup's success, leading to improved returns on investment.

An example of post investment support is connecting a portfolio company with the firm's LP Network. LPs often prove to be a rolodex of successful and connected investors that can help with various functions of business building. Furthermore, the better the VC does, the more money the LP makes which creates alignment. By managing a pipeline of portfolio company needs and connecting them with helpful LPs, a VC can drive positive investment outcomes. Particular action items could include a strategic partnership between a consumer good portfolio company and an LP that is an executive at Walmart, connecting a unicorn in the fintech sector that needs a CFO with an LP who has hired a fintech CFO before, or connecting a financing company in need of a Series C investor to a prominent growth equity shop. Managing these post investment requests may seem thankless at times, but making the right connection could end up being the task that catapults a young VC up the ranks.

Continuous Learning and Adaptability

By actively engaging in platform support, young VCs expose themselves to the nitty-gritty of business operations, challenges, and strategies across diverse sectors. This immersion allows them to build a wider network, spot industry trends, and adapt to the rapidly changing startup landscape, making them more effective investors. Consider a young VC that is incubating an investment in the sports media industry. The startup founders are highly creative and have bootstrapped their business to becoming an award winning brand. They have no financial background and are unsure on how to build a proper operating model to refine forecasting as they shift focus to user growth and monetization. A junior investor with a finance background tirelessly builds the operating model for the founders, works with them on the forecasting assumptions, and teaches them how to use the model until the day comes that they are big enough for a finance hire. Through this experience, the investor gains valuable insights into the sports media industry, including an understanding of paid acquisition tactics, hands-on forecasting, and budgeting experience for growing businesses. These skills not only helped the sports media company in our case, but would develop transferable learnings for the investor to bring to future investment opportunities.

Expanding Networks

A VC's network is one of their most powerful assets. Through platform support, VCs naturally expand their connections to include not just founders and co-investors, but also industry experts, potential customers, and key hires. These relationships, cultivated over time, can lead to new deal flow, partnerships, and insights that might be inaccessible to those not deeply engaged in platform activities. Consider an investor's relationships with startup vendors through a recommended vendor program. Vendor programs are time consuming but important initiatives for ensuring your portfolio companies are successful. For example, developing relationships with highly reputable VC lawyers is a valuable way to ensure your portfolio companies receive the best possible legal support, and potentially a platform level discount. In addition, these lawyers maintain relationships with other VC's and in-demand startups. Those connections may lead to your next big investment opportunity or even later stage funding for one of your portfolio companies. A platform professional's deep relationships with vendors can be a difference maker for success.

In conclusion, while capital deployment remains a fundamental aspect of venture capital, the landscape is shifting towards a more holistic approach where value addition is not just desirable but essential.

For the young VC looking to grow and thrive, focusing on platform support not only offers a competitive edge but also ensures they are actively contributing to the startup ecosystem. As they invest not just their funds but their time, knowledge, and network, they position themselves and their portfolio companies for success in an increasingly complex market.

Day 5: **How to contribute to exits**

Deek Velagandula – Waverley Capital

So it's time for one of your portfolio companies to think about an exit – perhaps it's a scaled business looking to tap the public markets, or a rocketship receiving inbound interest from strategic, or unfortunately a plateauing / declining business looking to return some value for its employees and investors. While each of these scenarios carries vastly different strategic priorities and negotiating angles, there are a number of common considerations that are useful across scenarios. These are helpful primarily to ensure that the company / founder retains negotiating leverage and that all parties (founders / employees / investors) remain aligned throughout the process.

Get an advisor!

Unless the maximum exit valuation of your portfolio company is expected to be sub $50M, the importance and power of a quality M&A advisor is incomparable. Investment bankers often get a bad rap in the venture capital community, often for shilling low quality deal flow or taking exorbitant fees on money raised. Where a good banker earns their money is in running a tight M&A or IPO process, ensuring that a comprehensive set of strategic and financial investors are involved in the potential acquisition and that each has the appropriate amount of pressure and leverage applied to them. That being said, the job of your banker is to manage the universe of potential acquirers, and the job of your portfolio founder / executive is to manage your advisors. Be sure to set clear stage-gates and timelines to avoid unexpected cash-out situations or long, tedious M&A processes.

Avoid the 'wink-wink' deal

Particularly when there is inbound M&A interest from major strategic or key customers, founders often believe they can handle these conversations based on their previous relationships or knowledge. Rather, corporate development teams and seasoned private equity investors (and even venture capitalists for that matter) are notorious for being one-foot-in, one-foot-out regularly for the purposes of gathering information and preserving optionality. This often leads to extremely detailed and time consuming due diligence, unclear "owners" on the part of the potential acquirer, and too often, a lack of a consummated transaction. Rather than continue to 'wink-wink' at an M&A process, founders are often best positioned when they make it clear that the company is exploring strategic options and that they'd love to have Company or Fund XYZ be a part of that process.

REALLY understand your portfolio founders' intentions and motivations

Just as VC investors diligence a founders commitment to building a potentially $B+ business when considering an investment, it is also imperative to be aligned on your founders' expectations and motivations when it comes to an exit. First, founders often have in their head a "minimum viable price", aka the lowest priced deal they would be happy with accepting. This may be an arbitrary goal number that they've had for a number of years, a number that enables them to live a certain life they want, or simply a number they feel they deserve for the years of blood and sweat put into building the business. Regardless of motivation, knowing that number as a board member of investor goes a long way in understanding what type of deal will get done, and how much negotiating a founder will be wiling to do. Second, strategic and cultural fit are imperative in finding the ideal home for your portfolio company. Spend time with your founders to understand where this might be – your job is to find the best home for the business in the long term. This may sometimes come at a lower initial price or valuation, but will go a long way in terms of your own reputation as well the founders / company's satisfaction and motivation following a transaction.

As a junior or rising VC, the amount of exposure you get to the Board and/or exit process may be limited. However, targeted advice and guidance such as the above can go a long way in punching above your weight within the firm.

WEEK 9

FOLLOW ONS / GROWTH STAGE INVESTING

Day 1: **What is different in growth stage?**

Jack Harvey - Causeway

A lot of time, energy, and verbiage is spent on defining stage (pre-seed, seed, seed-extension, post-seed, Early Series A, Late Series A, Series B, C, D, etc.). Silicon Valley Bank does a great job here[29] outlining the various investment rounds in Venture Capital. It is important to familiarize yourself with this terminology, the common characteristics of companies raising a particular round, and the different funding sources. However, the reality is that the specific nomenclature used to define fundraising rounds, and thus the attributes of a company raising said round, change with time. It's not that terms like "Seed" or "Series A" aren't important – they are – but these distinctions have blurry lines. As a result, I think it's more helpful to orient your understanding of "stage" around the fundamental characteristics of a business vs. some ever-changing naming process or arbitrary measurement of dollars raised. We will focus our discussion here on the "growth stage", what it is, and how it is different than "early stage" investing.

So, what is a "growth stage" company? A growth stage company is one that has already built the machinery of growth and can prove that it is working. They have a product in market and have significant customer and revenue traction. The company is no longer pitching a dream about the future. Instead, they are pitching an actual operating company with historical performance data. For clarity's sake, this is typically after the company has raised a sizable amount of capital, usually from early stage VCs in the form of a "Series A"

---

[29] https://www.svb.com/startup-insights/vc-relations/stages-of-venture-capital

round. In other words, if a company is raising a Series B (or any letter that follows B in the alphabet), you're probably, but not definitely, looking at a growth stage company.

While a growth stage company has ideally made real progress towards profitability, it is likely still burning cash at an unsustainable rate. This cash burn can often be attributed to an unwavering focus on revenue growth and capturing market share. As opposed to early stage companies, who raise capital to develop a business concept, create a product, or begin generating sales, when growth stage companies raise money, they are focused on expanding an existing set of activities that are already working. More specifically:

- Further developing existing products or services (e.g., adding new features)

- Expanding into new markets to reach new customers

- Hiring more salespeople and filling important management team openings

- Spending more on marketing

Because a growth stage company has already obtained substantial traction, it is significantly de-risked. This has two major impacts for investors: 1) the amount of capital available is considerably higher, usually leading to greater investor competition, and 2) the potential return on an investment is lower.

The investor base for growth stage companies is large and growing. There are growth stage-specific VCs, traditional private equity firms, hedge funds, family offices, sovereign wealth funds, banks, ultra-high net worth individuals...the list goes on. All of these parties have significantly more capital to deploy. As a result, the investment process is highly competitive and usually facilitated by a more formal process than at earlier stages. What industry-specific value-add do you bring to the company? Do you require a board seat? How much are you willing to invest? How does your proposed valuation compare to other investors? These are questions that founders ask whenever they are raising money, but they are even more important at the growth stage. The power balance shifts from investors to founders as companies prove themselves and move on to their next phase of growth. It's important to understand this dynamic as an investor.

Growth stage companies are already doing lots of things well when they go out to raise more capital. The focus then for investors is to identify those early data points and growth levers. As a result, investors spend more time evaluating actual historical operating metrics. This often comes in the form of combing through user and/or customer data, growth, retention, and churn. While this can be true at the early stages, growth stage companies simply have more data available. This allows investors to take a more informed view on the business and have greater certainty about how additional capital will accelerate growth. The team, product, and market opportunity are just as important for a Series C round as they are for a Seed round, but now you just have more information to make an investment decision.

Day 2: **What needs to happen for a follow on?**

Juliette Rolnick - BDMI Fund

VCs typically know when the time is coming for them to make that final follow-on investment decision.

Maybe they've been strategizing with the company and other investors in board meetings on when exactly to go out for another raise, lukewarm on the future of the business. Or maybe they've been eagerly staying in touch with the founder, hoping to get a super pro-rata allocation on the subsequent round that they know most VCs would be eager to partake in, if they only had the chance.

The follow-on investment decision is a nuanced one. It's not just about whether or not the company has hit or exceeded its targets for the past few quarters or how the company's weighted pipeline looks. Rather, there's a host of follow-on deal dynamics which are crucial to consider when making this decision, as this decision has the potential to rapidly excite growth in a company within which you've already put capital to work, or it can turn a hero into a zero.

First, let's think through some of the questions that are important to ask oneself in considering the future success of the business itself:

- Has the company achieved the metrics and KPIs that they said they would at the time of the initial investment?

    o Note that if the answer here is no, it is not automatically negative. In fact, I've seen scenarios in which VCs are eager to do their super pro-rata and simply attribute any financial and KPI misses to poor forecasting.

- Do I believe that the business is underpriced at its current valuation and will bring higher returns once more capital is put to work?

  o If the answer is yes and depending on how undervalued the VC perceives the company as, the VC may opt to do their super pro rata (more than their initial investment share). If the deal is exciting, this opportunity may get competitive amongst insiders.

Beyond evaluating the overall excitement of the business, there are some subtle and not-so-subtle deal dynamics that should be considered when follow-on investing. These mostly come into play when thinking about *not* following-on:

- If I can be expected to invest now, how will it be perceived by other (primarily outside) investors if I decide not to follow-on invest?

  o There are certainly investors who cannot be expected to participate in future financing rounds. Perhaps these investors focus on earlier stages, making a later-stage growth round not a fit.

  o That said, if you're an investor who can be expected to invest at least your pro-rata, then why wouldn't you maintain your percentage ownership, unless the business is just not that exciting? This would be perceived by outsiders as poor signaling, decreasing the likelihood for a company to successfully pull a round together and attract the capital needed to return the investment you've already made. Signaling matters, and VCs will often invest their pro-rata for that purpose, if not much else.

- What rights might I lose if I don't invest my pro-rata?

  o Non-participating, existing investors may lose some or all of their preferential rights, including anti-dilution protections, liquidation preferences, or voting rights, when "pay-to-play" provisions are put in place. This is often in the context of a "down" round, when a subset of existing investors is incentivizing insider participation.

Overall, positive investor signaling is very important in the world of venture capital, in which metrics and financials are hardly audited. VCs only know how well things are going at a startup via conversations had and actions witnessed, and we all know that actions speak louder than words.

Day 3: **How to conduct cohort analysis**

Andrew Ciatto - Ribbit Capital

- *What is customer cohort analysis?*

    o   To make investment and operating decisions, investors and operators often look at customer cohorts – buckets of customers based on when they were acquired – to see how KPIs are trending over time.

    For example, a software company may want to understand how spending changed for customers who joined in January 2019 over their next 12 months and if that trend improved, worsened, or stayed the same for customers acquired in January 2021 and their subsequent 12 months. While some "degradation" is expected over time because most businesses go after their ideal customers first (most willing to pay, desire to spend more...etc), a business that experiences consistent or even improving cohort performance over time is on to something special.

- *Why is cohort analysis important?*

    o   Retention is one of the most important characteristics investors look for (especially in companies that have found Product Market Fit), and cohort analysis is arguably the most comprehensive way to come to a granular POV on retention. When underwriting growth rates over a longer period of time (what many tech investors index valuation frameworks around for money-losing, high operating leverage businesses!), OK vs. good vs. great retention makes a huge difference. A business with 90% net dollar retention will need to "re-find" 10% of its revenue in net new customers each year *just to not decline top-line*. On the flip side, a business with 130% net dollar retention can grow 30% each year without having to add a single new customer. Similarly, businesses with strong retention tend to have very strong sales efficiency, because they rely less on their ability to spend S&M dollars to acquire net new customers, and more on their product's ability to keep and grow its users.

- *What are the different types of cohorts?*

  o As alluded to above, "retention" is one of the key metrics that an investor/operator can understand using cohorts. There are multiple kinds of retention and there are other KPIs that can be understood using cohort analysis as well. The type of cohort analyses that you conduct are based on the company's business model. For an enterprise software company, you may explore three kinds of retention - (1) logo retention, (2) gross retention, and (3) net dollar retention.

  o Logo retention is a 0-100% scale calculated as the number of customers in period 2 that started in period 1 (number of starting customers in period 1) – it does not consider new customers acquired between period 1 and 2. Practically speaking, if I start with 50 logos on Jan 1, 2021 and I finish the year with 45 of those same logos, I have 90% logo retention (even if I add 10 new customers in 2021 and finish the year with 55 aggregate customers)

  o Gross retention is similar, but instead of logos, it is dollar spend. It does not consider new customers AND it does not consider any upsell from those customers. For example, if I have 2 customers, one who spends $8K/year and one who spends $2K/year, if I lose the $2K customer, I had 50% logo retention, but I will have 80% gross dollar retention.

o Net dollar retention is the same as gross, but it accounts for upsell/cross-sell where existing customers in period 1 may increase their spend in period 2, so net retention can be greater than 100%. In the example above, if the $8K customer goes on to spend $15K and the $2K customer churns and spends zero, we have grown from a total of $10K to $15K, so logo retention is 50%, gross dollar retention is 80%, but net dollar retention is 150%.

o For a B2C business, it is helpful to look at customer retention across different usage behaviors (could be defined as making a purchase or logging in to an app) as well as other KPIs suited to the type of B2C business (looking at order frequency and average order value for an e-commerce site or looking at time spent or sessions per day per user for a mobile app).

- *Basics of cohort modeling:*

  o **Receive data** – Comes in different forms (could be an output of Stripe payments received from that month with customer IDs, or in a company-formatted template). The company may have 100 customers labeled ID 1-100, and they may have been in business from January 2018 to December 2020.

  o **Bucket customers into cohorts** - The goal here is to delineate what defines a specific cohort. Often this is done by using an excel formula (like INDEX MATCH) to identify the first month in which a customer starts using and/or paying for the product (first month with a non-zero value). You now have a long list with columns that include customer ID, spend each month, and a column that defines which cohort they are in. *[see below chart – rightmost column is an index match formula that finds out which quarter a customer started paying in]*

	Q1 2018	Q2 2018	Q3 2018	Q4 2018	Q1 2019	Q2 2019	Q3 2019	Q4 2019	Q1 2020	Q2 2020	Q3 2020	Q4 2020	Cohort
Name002	0	0	0	0	0	0	403,000	403,000	1,224,420	1,224,420	1,416,200	1,416,200	Q3 2019
Name003	0	0	0	0	0	0	0	0	0	1,382,400	1,382,400	1,382,400	Q2 2020
Name005	695,000	695,000	1,155,738	1,536,828	1,518,006	2,293,006	2,293,006	2,193,006	2,193,006	1,287,500	1,287,500	1,287,500	Q3 2016
Name008	0	0	105,000	469,583	469,583	469,583	469,583	469,583	364,583	364,583	950,611	950,611	Q3 2018
Name010	0	0	0	0	0	832,000	832,000	832,000	832,000	832,000	832,000	892,000	Q2 2019
Name026	0	596,000	596,000	596,000	596,000	596,000	596,000	818,500	818,500	818,500	818,500	818,500	Q2 2018
Name011	0	516,900	516,900	516,900	516,900	417,900	857,900	857,900	974,322	974,322	818,322	818,322	Q2 2018
Name013	0	0	200,475	200,475	200,475	200,475	240,875	812,475	812,475	899,144	906,370	806,370	Q3 2018
Name017	51,441	51,441	51,441	51,441	102,935	102,935	102,935	102,935	113,664	113,664	99,097	747,350	Q3 2017
Name015	686,029	767,186	767,186	861,486	861,486	861,486	666,644	666,644	752,491	752,491	602,491	725,403	Q3 2016
Name028	0	0	0	0	0	0	0	0	555,487	555,487	555,487	555,487	Q1 2020
Name029	199,000	199,000	199,000	199,000	549,000	549,000	549,000	549,000	549,000	549,000	549,000	549,000	Q3 2017
Name032	0	0	0	0	0	0	0	0	510,228	510,228	510,228	510,228	Q1 2020

o **Create cohort "table"** – The next step is to have a table with rows and columns from Q1 2018 to Q4 2020. The top left cell (Q1 2018 x Q1 2018) should call a "sumifs" function of the spend in Q1 2018 for any customer who is in the Q1 2018 cohort. This will help determine net retention for each cohort. Use "countifs" function for logo retention.

Net Retention

	Q1 2018	Q2 2018	Q3 2018	Q4 2018	Q1 2019	Q2 2019	Q3 2019	Q4 2019	Q1 2020	Q2 2020	Q3 2020	Q4 2020
Q1 2018	1110842	1110842	1110842	1256266.4	1347472.6	1486294.9	1509794.9	1546341.3	1524181.8	1535194.7	1535194.7	1561137
Q2 2018	0	2659558.3	2700541.8	2700541.8	2717922.3	2565252.7	3120274.9	3445793.2	3544215.2	3299237.2	3035755.9	2995862.5
Q3 2018	0	0	1864276.4	2278859.7	2278859.7	2273032.4	2254004	3110195.5	2843320.5	2941138	3525652.4	3386017.7
Q4 2018	0	0	0	2452483.1	2452483.1	2601859.5	2634657.8	2635461.7	2621580.8	2802029.6	2845948	2728090.2
Q1 2019	0	0	0	0	1489920.6	1497506.8	1538516.5	1538608.3	1544248.4	1635779	1694686	1685798.6
Q2 2019	0	0	0	0	0	3546714.6	3710199.9	3905059.7	3922252.4	3649571.2	3742195.1	3619747
Q3 2019	0	0	0	0	0	0	3230538.7	3230538.7	4170425.9	4513951.9	4320103.1	4378844.4
Q4 2019	0	0	0	0	0	0	0	4012129.7	4278129.7	4278129.7	4278129.7	4530783.1
Q1 2020	0	0	0	0	0	0	0	0	3040501.7	3039592	3071992	3134392
Q2 2020	0	0	0	0	0	0	0	0	0	3551154.8	3801168.8	3863168.8
Q3 2020	0	0.	0	0	0	0	0	0	0	0	1503118.2	1591120.9
Q4 2020	0	0	0	0	0	0	0	0	0	0	0	4959324.6

o **Offset function** – Your table above should have one cohort with data from Q0 to present, another cohort with Q1 to present, Q2 to present....etc. In order to compare apples to apples, use the offset function so that all cohorts are aligned with your leftmost column

	Q1	Q2	Q3	Q4	Q5	Q6	Q7	Q8	Q9	Q10	Q11	Q12
10 Q1 2018	1,110,842	1,110,842	1,110,842	1,256,265	1,347,473	1,486,295	1,509,795	1,546,341	1,524,182	1,535,195	1,535,195	1,561,137
11 Q2 2018	2,659,558	2,700,542	2,700,542	2,717,922	2,565,253	3,120,275	3,445,793	3,544,215	3,299,237	3,035,756	2,995,863	0
12 Q3 2018	1,864,276	2,278,860	2,278,860	2,273,032	2,254,004	3,110,195	2,843,320	2,941,138	3,525,652	3,386,018	0	0
13 Q4 2018	2,452,483	2,452,483	2,601,859	2,634,658	2,635,462	2,621,581	2,802,030	2,845,948	2,728,090	0	0	0
14 Q1 2019	1,489,921	1,497,507	1,538,516	1,538,608	1,544,248	1,635,779	1,694,686	1,685,799	0	0	0	0
15 Q2 2019	3,546,715	3,710,200	3,905,060	3,922,252	3,649,571	3,742,195	3,619,747	0	0	0	0	0
16 Q3 2019	3,230,539	3,230,539	4,170,426	4,513,952	4,320,103	4,378,844	0	0	0	0	0	0
17 Q4 2019	4,012,130	4,278,130	4,278,130	4,278,130	4,530,783	0	0	0	0	0	0	0
18 Q1 2020	3,040,502	3,039,592	3,071,992	3,134,392	0	0	0	0	0	0	0	0
19 Q2 2020	3,551,155	3,801,169	3,863,169	0	0	0	0	0	0	0	0	0
20 Q3 2020	1,503,118	1,591,121	0	0	0	0	0	0	0	0	0	0
21 Q4 2020	4,959,325	0	0	0	0	0	0	0	0	0	0	0

o **% Output** – Next, you want to figure out how each cohort has trended over time by indexing around the spend (or logos, usage, etc) that each specific cohort exhibited in their first month with the product. To calculate this, divide each figure (from period 2 onwards) by period 1.

Net Retention

	Q1	Q2	Q3	Q4	Q5	Q6	Q7	Q8	Q9	Q10	Q11	Q12
Q1 2018	100%	100%	100%	113%	121%	134%	136%	139%	137%	138%	138%	141%
Q2 2018	100%	102%	102%	102%	96%	117%	130%	133%	124%	114%	113%	
Q3 2018	100%	122%	122%	122%	121%	167%	153%	158%	189%	182%		
Q4 2018	100%	100%	106%	107%	107%	107%	114%	116%	111%			
Q1 2019	100%	101%	103%	103%	104%	110%	114%	113%				
Q2 2019	100%	105%	110%	111%	103%	106%	102%					
Q3 2019	100%	100%	129%	140%	134%	136%						
Q4 2019	100%	107%	107%	107%	113%							
Q1 2020	100%	100%	101%	103%								
Q2 2020	100%	107%	109%									
Q3 2020	100%	106%										
Q4 2020	100%											
Weighted Average	100%	104%	110%	112%	112%	123%	121%	131%	137%	141%	120%	141%

o **Graph** – once you have the above set up, you can create graph outputs like the below using line charts

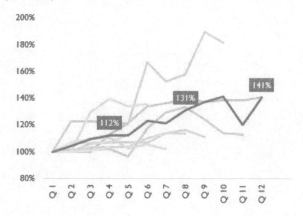

- *Common pitfalls to watch out for:*

  o *When you have a few* key customers responsible for a large part of the revenue, this may skew the retention.

  o Cohort "degradation" – it is important to take into account if cohort performance is getting better or worse over time coupled with the stage of the business. For businesses that are post-PMF, you want to see improving retention over time (as the product gets stronger). Many companies may have weaker retention earlier on by "casting too wide of a net" and selling their product to customers who are not in their "ideal customer persona". Businesses with network effects should also exhibit *stronger* customer retention at maturity.

Day 4: **SPVs: A detailed breakdown**

Erik de Stefanis - Interlace Ventures

The easiest way to explain Special Purpose Vehicle (SPV) and Syndicates is to first run through the associated terminology, and then to piece it all together.

You may have heard the terms SPV and Syndicate used interchangeably. But, I prefer to keep them separate.

Let's begin with the term **Syndicate.** In this context, a Syndicate is typically composed of a collective of angel investors, investing either independently or together. Family offices and funds can also invest through syndicates. These investors are referred to as Limited Partners, or LPs (defined in the next section). An LP can belong to multiple syndicates, and each syndicate is run/organized/managed by one or more Syndicate Leads. Typically, a Syndicate will have, and be known for, its own brand. Numerous syndicates have built their brand around expertise in a specific vertical, and there are syndicates consisting of alumni from various well-known tech companies (e.g. Door Dash Alumni Syndicate) investing together and bringing domain expertise to each deal.

An **LP** is a silent partner in a partnership (read more about partnerships here[30], and how they differ from LLCs here[31]). In a partnership, you typically have LPs and GPs (General Partners, also known as Managing Partners). This set-up is common for traditional venture funds. However, many SPVs are actually set-up as LLCs, where you

---

[30] https://www.investopedia.com/terms/l/limitedpartnership.asp

[31] https://www.legalzoom.com/articles/difference-between-llc-and-llp

don't have the LP/GP structure, but the terminology is still used when speaking about SPVs and Syndicates.

A **Syndicate Lead**, often referred to as a GP (General Partner), is an individual (or group of individuals) who sources the deal and manages a syndicate. Syndicate Leads will create a new SPV for each new investment. Leads will share investment opportunities with their syndicate, i.e. their LPs.

The purpose of SPVs or Special Purpose Vehicles is typically to pool funds from LPs and acquire (invest in) a specific asset (e.g. a startup). Think of an SPV as a one-deal venture fund with its own balance sheet. The SPV ultimately ends up on the cap-table as a single line item.

SPVs enable multiple investors to write smaller (sometimes as small as $1K) checks into private companies. VC funds usually have high minimum commitment amounts for LPs. SPVs enable investors with less capital to deploy to get exposure to this asset class. Although it is common for individuals, i.e. Syndicate Leads to utilize SPVs, it is also common for funds to use them for various purposes, such as allowing LPs to co-invest with the fund (through an SPV) in specific deals. Sometimes, when funds no longer have sufficient reserve capital for a follow-on investment in a later round, they'll use an SPV to fill their pro-rata instead of investing out of the fund.

Note: *Syndicates are almost always invite-only, however, some syndicates have thousands of LPs; whereas others have only a handful. Even larger syndicates will often be able to run more discreet processes should the founder in question ask that the materials (memo, deck) be shared with as few LPs as possible. Usually, such a raise will entail a higher minimum commitment amount from LPs.*

This is useful when the founder is concerned about the distribution of sensitive information and/or the optics of their raise.

SPVs appear on the cap-table the same way that typical funds do. The founder of the startup does not need to interact with the SPV's LPs the same way that a founder typically does not interact with the LPs of the funds on their cap-table. Below is a graphic demonstrating a cap-table with many smaller checks (left), and on the right is the same cap-table, but with the smaller checks pooled into an SPV. Pooling all these smaller checks into one vehicle saves the founder a lot of time that would otherwise be spent on chasing signatures and wires.

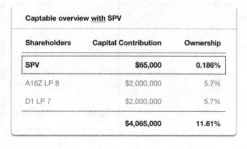

Captable overview without SPV

Shareholders	Capital Contribution	Ownership
Angel 1	$25,000	0.07%
Angel 2	$10,000	0.03%
Angel 3	$10,000	0.03%
Angel 4	$15,000	0.04%
Angel 5	$5,000	0.01%
A16Z LP 8	$2,000,000	5.7%
D1 LP 7	$2,000,000	5.7%
	$4,065,000	11.61%

Captable overview with SPV

Shareholders	Capital Contribution	Ownership
SPV	$65,000	0.186%
A16Z LP 8	$2,000,000	5.7%
D1 LP 7	$2,000,000	5.7%
	$4,065,000	11.61%

Cap-table without SPV vs Cap-table with same investors, but all angels grouped into an SPV

The graphic below shows multiple LPs investing various smaller sums into a single SPV, managed by the Syndicate Lead. The SPV then acquires shares in the target company.

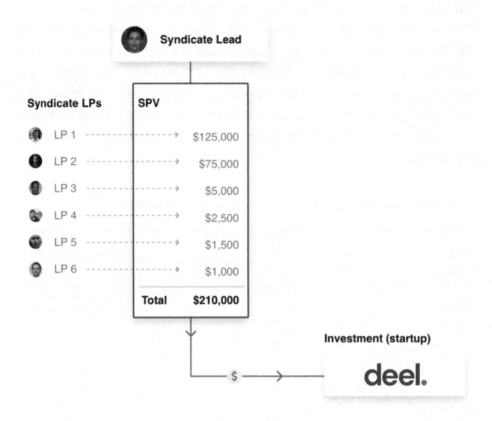

The graphic below demonstrates the dynamics of a Syndicate. The Syndicate Lead shares multiple investment opportunities with their LPs. LPs decide which deal(s) they want to participate in and invest only into those SPVs.

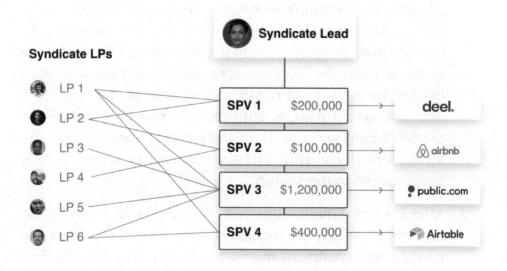

To sum things up, **Syndicate Leads** start, grow, and manage **Syndicates**. A Syndicate Lead will build a brand around their syndicate, the same way that VC funds have various brands or focuses, i.e. what they are known for, what they specialize in, etc. This helps with **LP** recruitment and deal flow. Once a Syndicate Lead has identified a target asset, and with full support and consent of the founder, the Syndicate Lead will set-up an **SPV** and share the investment opportunity with their LPs. The LPs that want to participate in the specific opportunity will commit capital to the SPV. Once the capital has been pooled into the SPV, the SPV will invest in the target asset (startup). The startup now has one additional row on their cap-table, the SPV entity (see below).

Here is more detailed breakdown of how this usually works (from the perspective of the Syndicate Lead).

1. **Get an allocation** – Once the Lead has completed their due diligence and has conviction in the deal, they will secure an

allocation in a startup's round. The Lead must be transparent with the founder about the SPV process (i.e. timeline, the need to share information among the Lead's LPs, etc.). Due to the fact that the Lead needs to raise the capital on a deal-by-deal basis, it is not possible to guarantee the founder a final investment amount until the LPs' money is actually in the SPV's bank account. The Lead typically does not sign any investment documents until the capital has arrived and is ready to wire to the startup.

2. **Memo** – Once the founder has given the Lead an allocation and both are aligned regarding the process, the Lead will prepare an investment memo to share with their LPs. The Lead is not selling an investment opportunity; it is sharing an opportunity that it is personally excited about. The founder should approve the memo before it is circulated among LPs.

3. **SPV formation** – This step can come either before or after circulating materials with LPs depending on how confident the Lead is that they will be able to raise capital for the deal. The Lead will most likely be using a third-party service for this (more on this in a later article). The process of forming an SPV and getting a bank account set-up usually takes anywhere from a few hours to a few days. Once this is complete, LPs will have the ability to commit to the deal (e-sign documents, wire commitments).

4. **Share with LPs** – Distribute the approved memo and deck among the LPs along with a deal-link (assuming the SPV is ready to accept commitments). LPs will review the opportunity, and those who are interested will be able to commit to the deal. All the admin work (collecting wires, generating documents, etc.) will be taken care of by the Lead's third-party SPV platform.

- **Close the deal.** Execute the fundraising documents between the SPV and the startup and wire the funds. This too is often done by the Lead's SPV admin platform.

Part 2: SPV Economics

LPs in a typical VC fund are usually charged "two and twenty" or "2/20". The "two" refers to an annual management fee, and the "twenty" refers to the carried interest, which is usually 20% of the returned capital (once LPs have received their principal back).

The **management fee** is typically calculated based on committed capital (although sometimes it is a function of called capital), i.e. the capital that LPs have committed to the fund. If a fund has $50M in total commitments, then a 2% management fee would equate to $1M per year for the lifetime of the fund (usually ~10 years for an early stage fund). $1M per year for 10 years equals $10M or 20% of the total fund. It is common for smaller funds to charge a higher management fee during the first few years and then gradually decrease it, but on average, the management fees will equate to 20% of the total amount raised by the fund. Management fees cover the fund's overhead, i.e. salaries, legal fees, etc.

Most VC funds will not call all the capital at once. The deployment period usually stretches over the course of several years and you don't want sleeping money, i.e. money that is not being put to work. **Capital calls** can occur at various cadences, e.g. quarterly, bi-yearly, etc. and at each capital call LPs will wire a portion of their total commitment to the fund.

SPVs are different. They have only one capital call or closing, i.e. LPs wire their full commitments to the SPV at once. Whether an SPV charges a management fee or not is up to the Syndicate Lead; many chose not to. However, some Leads charge a one-time management fee and others will charge an annual management fee. Out of the +100 SPVs that my team has run in the past year or so, our LPs have been subject to a one-time management fee on only three or four deals, all of which were +$1M SPVs. The reason was to cover costs incurred in addition to the typical set-up fee.

Carried Interest, often referred to simply as **carry**, is more or less a performance fee, i.e. a percentage of the LPs' profit, if there is any. The industry standard for early stage VC funds and SPVs is 20%. The GPs of a VC fund, or the Syndicate Lead of an SPV, will receive their carry after their LPs' principal investment has been returned. If the carry is 20%, then the GPs/Lead will receive 20% of all gains, less the LPs' principal.

As with VC funds, there are costs associated with establishing and managing an SPV. The costs include SPV formation, preparation of annual statements for LPs, state filing fees, etc. These fees can range from ~$2K on the low end up to tens of thousands on the high end, depending on your SPV service provider and the specific needs of your SPV. These costs are sometimes covered by the Lead. But, more commonly, they will be covered by all participating LPs on a pro-rata basis. Often these costs are one-time (at the time of creating the SPV), but each service provider has different cost structures.

Below is a walk-through of SPV economics (not taking fees into consideration)

A Syndicate Lead raises $200K for an SPV. Five years later, the company exits and the value of the SPV is now $1M. It generated a 5X return. First, the LPs get their money back, i.e. their principal. They collectively invested $200K, so we'll deduct $200K from $1M and are now left with $800K. Of the remaining $800K, 20%, or $160K, goes to the Lead as carry.

Below is a chart laying out various carry-outcomes for an SPV Lead, assuming a 20% carry. SPV Leads will often commit only a small percentage of the total amount raised by their SPV, often as little as $1K. This can potentially lead to misaligned incentives between Leads and their LPs.

SPV Lead's carry based on total amount raised and outcome:

SPV Raise Amount ↓	2X	3X	5X	10X	20X	100X
$50,000	$10,000	$20,000	$40,000	$90,000	$190,000	$990,000
$100,000	$20,000	$280,000	$480,000	$980,000	$1,980,000	$9,980,000
$200,000	$40,000	$80,000	$160,000	$360,000	$760,000	$3,960,000
$500,000	$100,000	$200,000	$400,000	$900,000	$1,900,000	$9,900,000
$1,000,000	$200,000	$400,000	$800,000	$1,800,000	$3,800,000	$19,800,000

Day 5: **What are the basics of financial modeling?**

Hammad Aslam – Susa Ventures

Before I jumped to venture capital, I used to work in private equity, where 50-tab models with thousands of lines are often table stakes. Rewind a bit further to my banking days and it was the same story. I started and ended my career in banking building complicated models for companies trying to get acquired.

But here's some good news for you: you won't have to do all that as a venture capital investor! Well, you'll still have to build models but the perspective offered by the model in a diligence process is totally different, which drastically reduces the necessity to build complicated models all the time. Sounds awesome, right? Well, let's get into it! (Btw, I am going to primarily talk about early and growth-stage financial modeling)

At Series B or C, it's incredibly difficult to articulate, at a granular level, all the possible paths a company could take. Quantifying all those possibilities can create false precision and take up your valuable time in the diligence process, with limited return. In my opinion, the best way is to articulate a "What do you need to believe case" using your best judgment of what it would take for an opportunity to hit the threshold returns you would expect. This way, you leverage your model to contextualize the rest of the diligence and can ask yourself if you believe the modeled outcome is possible, given everything you know about the company at that particular point in time. Additional bull or base cases can be qualitative or quantitative on top of the "what do you need to believe", based on one or two key variables that would have the highest impact on the story.

Building a "What-do-you-need-to-believe model"

Income Statement

Think about modeling a business on an annual or quarterly basis – anything more detailed is excessive, especially for high-growth companies. Your projection period should at least be (T+1) where T is the year of the liquidity event (my personal preference is 10 yr. forecast for additional flexibility)

The most important part of the model is to identify and focus on the most important KPIs of the company. These include but are not limited to customer count, ACV, retention rate, TPV, GMV, LTV: CAC, sales productivity, magic number, customer size, etc.

Create an outline of the model: figure out your key drivers – these will usually be the KPIs you have identified – and identify the best mechanic to project from a period-over-period basis. These mechanics can include growth rate, attach rate, ratios, averages, etc.

$ in thousands, unless noted otherwise	Annual		
	FY2020	FY2021	FY2022
Customer Snowball			
Beginning			
+ New			
- Churn			
+ / - Start / Stop			
Ending Customers			
PoP Growth (%)			
Annualized Growth (%)			
iCAGR (%)			
Average Customers			
PoP Growth (%)			
Customer Retention (%)			
ARR Snowball			
Beginning			
+ New			
+ Upsell			
- Downsell / Churn			
Ending ARR			
PoP Growth (%)			
Annualized Growth (%)			
iCAGR (%)			
Average ARR			
PoP Growth (%)			
Snowball Metrics (Annualized)			
New Bookings Growth (%) PoP			
Gross Retention (%)			
Net Retention (%)			
Upsell as % of Beginning (%)			
Key Metrics			
Average Customer Size			
Average New Customer			
Average Lost Customer			
New Size Factor			
Attrition Size Factor			

Exhibit: Sample key drivers for a software company

Once you have your outline, start with your KPIs and project them out based on the drivers. Don't shortcut the process by just projecting revenue on a growth rate – maybe you end up landing at the same spot by driving revenue/margins through KPI projection, but the latter approach will give you a lot more visibility and control over how and why certain KPIs impact the outlook of the business.

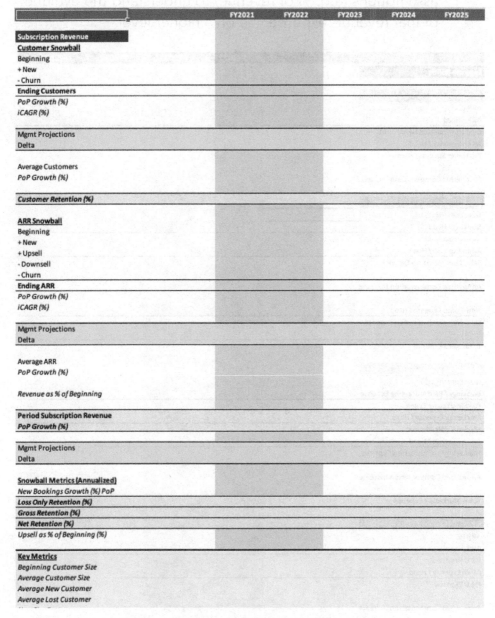

Exhibit: Sample projection levers for a software company

- These KPIs will then translate into the income statement for you. For lines where you don't have a lot of visibility or don't have a granular perspective, think about using simplified assumptions (e.g. % of revenue) to understand the evolution of that revenue/expense line on a higher level.

	FY2021	FY2022	FY2023	FY2024
Expense Builds				
Customer Success				
ARR ($)				
ARR / Head				
Customer Success Headcount				
All-in Expense / Head				
Customer Success Expense				
Annualized Compensation Increase				
Sales				
New Bookings ($)				
Booking / Head ($)				
Sales Headcount				
All-in Expense / Head				
Sales Compensation Expense				
Annualized Compensation Increase				
Non-Comp Expense / Head				
Sales Non-Compensation Expense				
Total Sales Expense				
Marketing				
New Bookings ($)				
Bookings / Paid Marketing Expense				
Paid Marketing Expense				
Marketing Expense / Head				
Marketing Headcount				
All-in Expense / Head				
Marketing Compensation Expense				
Annualized Compensation Increase				
Total Marketing Expense				
R&D				
ARR ($)				
ARR / Head				
R&D Headcount				
All-in Expense / Head				
R&D Expense				
Annualized Compensation Increase				

Exhibit: Drivers for income statement metrics

- Think about implied checks on your base case to test your assumptions. A great example of such an implied check is implied market penetration (projected revenue/TAM) or sales metrics (productivity, magic number, LTV: CAC, etc.). A lot of times, implied checks are just KPIs that you did not use to drive your projections. Alternatively, you can also think about the company relative to the rest of the industry (would this make you the first, fifth, 10th biggest company?) and if you are comfortable with those conclusions.

- There are some rules-of-thumb that you can expect in most situations, to test the precision of your model (of course, there can be exceptions to these rules, but they are more situation-dependent). Some examples include:

  o Top line growth rate tends to decrease over time until you reach normalized growth rates. Broadly, Long-term GDP growth is considered as the baseline but companies can take a long time to get there (many tech companies still have not after 20+ years)

  o Margins tend to scale up as operating leverage and scale improves

  o Multiples tend to decline as top-line growth declines

  o All else equal, extending the investment horizon will decrease IRR

- For an early-stage company, 80% of the time, there is no need to project out a balance sheet or an income statement. Unless you are focused on an asset-heavy business, balance sheet-based business, physical hardware, etc. there are minimal investment highlights that you can gain from detailed balance statements or cash flow builds.

  o Sometimes, it can be helpful to project cash through investment horizon but use your best judgment on that

- Try to keep your model as simple as possible. Compact models, limited hardcodes, organized flowthrough, proper formatting, and color-coding will be incredibly valuable to you and your team. You should build models with the expectation that a stranger can open your model and understand how it works in 15 mins.

- You can pull multiples from databases (CapIQ, SNL, etc.), industry margins and KPIs from public financials (10-Q's, 10-K's, S-1s, etc). These can all be directly relevant to your model or serve as good sanity checks.

Calculating Valuation and Returns

Finally! Let's get to the good stuff – this is what everyone on your team (including you) will be focused on:

- There are many different valuation methodologies out there: My recommendation would be to skip DCFs and use public company or transaction comparables to value a business

  o DCFs are imprecise for early-stage companies because, at that stage, it is extremely difficult to get an accurate, intrinsic valuation. Most of the equity value ends up buried in the terminal value, which negates the point of doing a DCF. DCFs also tend to be highly sensitive to discount rates and WACCs can be difficult to calculate for early-stage private companies

- Find out other business models that are good comparable companies for a business – when you can't find perfect comps, use a basket than can be a good approximation for what the public market would use to evaluate the business, or use a Sum-of-the-Parts approach to use different sets of comps for specific pieces of the business.

7-Jan-22		EV / Gross profit			EV / Gross profit / growth			GP CAGR	GP Margin	7-Jan-22		
		2021E	2022E	2023E	2021E	2022E	2023E	2021E-23E	2021E-23E	Share price	Market cap	EV
AvidXchange		14.6x	11.9x	9.5x	0.6x	0.5x	0.4x	24%	62%	$13.21	$2,698	$2,155
Coupa Software		21.9x	18.1x	14.5x	1.0x	0.8x	0.6x	23%	72%	$137.61	$10,277	$11,244
Paymentus		25.9x	20.2x	15.4x	0.9x	0.7x	0.5x	30%	80%	$28.27	$3,393	$3,263
Flywire		24.7x	19.1x	14.6x	0.8x	0.6x	0.5x	30%	70%	$33.11	$3,466	$3,043
Engagesmart		19.2x	14.7x	11.2x	0.6x	0.5x	0.4x	31%	78%	$21.16	$3,421	$3,168
Billtrust		8.2x	6.8x	5.6x	0.4x	0.3x	0.3x	21%	73%	$6.69	$1,063	$775
Average		19.1x	15.1x	11.8x	0.7x	0.6x	0.4x	26%	72%			
Block (Square)		14.8x	11.5x	9.0x	0.5x	0.4x	0.3x	28%	87%	$141.54	$65,289	$65,139
Shopify		54.5x	42.3x	32.0x	1.8x	1.4x	1.1x	30%	54%	$1,144.48	$143,718	$137,300
Marqeta		34.4x	27.8x	21.6x	1.3x	1.1x	0.8x	26%	42%	$15.57	$8,410	$7,310
Adyen		61.9x	44.0x	32.7x	1.6x	1.2x	0.9x	38%	100%	€ 2,145.00	€ 66,374	€ 63,116
Average		41.4x	31.4x	23.8x	1.3x	1.0x	0.8x	31%	71%			
Average		28.0x	21.6x	16.6x	1.0x	0.7x	0.6x	28%	72%			
Median		23.3x	18.6x	14.6x	0.8x	0.7x	0.5x	29%	72%			
Bill.com	Current $201.93	61.0x	35.5x	25.5x	1.1x	0.7x	0.5x	55%	82%	$201.93	$21,407	$20,667
	Target $339.00	103.9x	60.5x	43.5x	1.9x	1.1x	0.8x	55%	82%	$339.00	$35,949	$35,210

7-Jan-22		EV / Sales			EV / Sales / growth			CAGR	
		2021	2022	2023	2021	2022	2023	2020-23	Source
AvidXchange		8.8x	7.3x	6.1x	0.4x	0.4x	0.3x	20%	VA
Coupa Software		15.7x	12.9x	10.5x	0.7x	0.6x	0.5x	22%	VA
Paymentus		20.8x	15.9x	12.3x	0.7x	0.5x	0.4x	30%	VA
Flywire		17.3x	13.3x	10.3x	0.6x	0.4x	0.3x	30%	VA
Engagesmart		14.9x	11.5x	8.8x	0.5x	0.4x	0.3x	30%	VA
Billtrust		5.9x	5.0x	4.1x	0.3x	0.2x	0.2x	20%	VA
Average		20.3x	15.4x	11.8x	0.7x	0.5x	0.4x	28%	
Median		15.3x	12.2x	9.6x	0.6x	0.4x	0.3x	29%	
Bill.com	Current $201.93	50.3x	28.0x	21.0x	0.9x	0.5x	0.4x	55%	
	Target $339.00	85.7x	49.2x	35.8x	1.6x	0.9x	0.7x	55%	

Exhibit: Bill.com comps from Goldman Sachs Equity Research

- Understand what the public comps trade on – every business is going to have several multiples. Revenue, gross profit, growth-adjusted revenue, growth-adjusted gross profit, EBITDA, SS EBITDA, Net Income, SS Net Income, Free Cash Flow, Bookings, TPV, GMV can all be denominators for multiple. Your job is to figure out which ones the market looks at and which ones are implied.

- Identify when you expect the liquidity event to happen – this can be based on getting to a certain scale or a certain financial profile that is palatable for public market investors.

- Identify the time horizon of the key metric (for the multiple): Most often, you will go with NTM (next twelve months) or (Current Year + 1) / 1-year forward metrics.

- There are two schools of thought on how to apply these multiples to the company in question:

  o Approach 1: Use the average of historically normalized comps multiples (ex. 5-yr or 10-yr avg.) to the relevant metric(s) at the time of the projected liquidity event

  o Approach 2: Use the average of current comps multiples to the relevant multiple metrics at the time of the projected liquidity event

    - I am a strong proponent of the first approach: Ultimately, we are investing with extremely long-time horizons and as much as we would love to, we cannot predict the future. Public markets (or acquisition trends) will always fluctuate – we have no idea if 2025 will be a bull or a bear market (sure, we have our guesses, but no one can offer a prediction with a high level of confidence). With this level of uncertainty, the best approach is to take the historical performance of the market and use a normalized average of that. This also adds an air of conservatism to your model and prevents pricing something at the top of the market. (This is also why I don't think current multiples should impact how early-stage companies get priced in private markets)

- Use your projected metrics and chosen multiple(s) to calculate the expected value of the business at the liquidity event. Don't forget to account for dilution from subsequent rounds, which will impact your returns. Folks use all kinds of different estimates for dilution (I have seen everything from 2% annually to 8% annually and 20%-55% cumulative). Use your best judgment based on stage, size, and future capital requirements to apply this discount.

	FY2021	FY2022	FY2023	FY2024	FY2025	FY2026	FY2027	FY2028	FY2029
Ending ARR	$1,000	$5,000	$15,000	$35,000	$65,000	$105,000	$145,000	$185,000	$225,000
YoY Growth (%)		400.0%	200.0%	133.3%	85.7%	61.5%	38.1%	27.6%	21.6%
Total Revenue	$1,000	$5,000	$15,000	$35,000	$65,000	$105,000	$145,000	$185,000	$225,000
YoY Growth (%)		400.0%	200.0%	133.3%	85.7%	61.5%	38.1%	27.6%	21.6%
NTM Revenue	$5,000	$15,000	$35,000	$65,000	$105,000	$145,000	$185,000	$225,000	$265,000
NTM Revenue Growth	400.0%	200.0%	133.3%	85.7%	61.5%	38.1%	27.6%	21.6%	17.8%
Valuation & Susa Returns									
NTM AV / Revenue	10.0x	10.0x	10.0x	10.0x	10.0x	10.0x	10.0x	10.0x	10.0x
AV / LTM ARR	50.0x	30.0x	23.3x	18.6x	16.2x	13.8x	12.8x	12.2x	11.8x
Enterprise Value ($MM)	$50.0	$150.0	$350.0	$650.0	$1,050.0	$1,450.0	$1,850.0	$2,250.0	$2,650.0
Net Debt ($MM)	$0.0	$0.0	$0.0	$0.0	$0.0	$0.0	$0.0	$0.0	$0.0
Equity Value ($MM)	$50.0	$150.0	$350.0	$650.0	$1,050.0	$1,450.0	$1,850.0	$2,250.0	$2,650.0
Years since Investment		Annual	1	2	3	4	5	6	7
Dilution		8.0%	92.0%	84.6%	77.9%	71.6%	65.9%	60.6%	55.8%
Cumulative Dilution			8.0%	15.4%	22.1%	28.4%	34.1%	39.4%	44.2%
Equity Value ($MM) post-Dilution			$322.0	$550.2	$817.6	$1,038.8	$1,219.3	$1,364.3	$1,478.3

Exhibit: Hypothetical example of calculating future equity value

- Using a range of entry valuation, calculate your expected return based on the calculated future value. This can be done on both a CoC (cash-over-cash) or an IRR basis. Feel free to add sensitivities around key assumptions (entry price, multiple, revenue growth, margins, etc.) to see how they impact your return profile.

	FY2024	FY2025	FY2026	FY2027	FY2028	FY2029
Post-Money Entry Valuation ($MM)			MoM (x)			
$100 MM	5.5x	8.2x	10.4x	12.2x	13.6x	14.8x
$125 MM	4.4x	6.5x	8.3x	9.8x	10.9x	11.8x
$150 MM	3.7x	5.5x	6.9x	8.1x	9.1x	9.9x
$175 MM	3.1x	4.7x	5.9x	7.0x	7.8x	8.4x
$200 MM	2.8x	4.1x	5.2x	6.1x	6.8x	7.4x
$225 MM	2.4x	3.6x	4.6x	5.4x	6.1x	6.6x
$250 MM	2.2x	3.3x	4.2x	4.9x	5.5x	5.9x
$275 MM	2.0x	3.0x	3.8x	4.4x	5.0x	5.4x
Step: $25 MM						

Exhibit: MoM calculation for hypothetical future equity value

Bringing it All Together

- Models are never accurate – you may get it right for a couple of quarters, but you will always have variability in actual performance vs. what you thought a business would do. This does not mean that modeling is useless unless it's 100% accurate. Ultimately, it is your opinion of what a base (optimistic) case would look like, given the limited information you have at any given point in time.

- Use the model as a lens to understand the rest of your diligence. Ask yourself: Do you believe that the company can hit X users or Y% retention rate by 2027? What is your level of conviction on that assertion and where is that conviction coming along? Having a clear perspective on the reasons why you think a company can deliver on expectations (that you are setting) is way more important than the actual numbers.

- Models, on their own, do not make or break deals. They give you an essential perspective to piece together the story. Don't think of the model as the central tenant of your diligence.

Some Concluding Tips

- When unsure about how to structure your model, look at the company's model (if provided) or look at equity research models for similar business models

- Leverage company materials to understand KPIs and how to effectively break them into relevant drivers

- Create excel template(s) to minimize the amount of work it would take to build a model from scratch

- **Always** leverage the financial diligence you have done in building your model – if you are looking at a software company and you have already done a retention analysis, use that as the basis for your model

- When in doubt, google it – you'll always find helpful answers

- Try to finish the first draft of your model (80% - 90%) of the time in 2 hours. This time limit will push you to keep it simple. Refining assumptions after the first pass takes time and it's time well spent to refine your opinion.

WEEK 10

MISCELLANEOUS

Day 1: **How to cultivate your LP network**

Matt Weinberg - Max Ventures

Almost anyone who hopes to make a go at a career in VC will eventually have to fundraise and develop investor (i.e. Limited Partner) relationships. But we know the LP world can be opaque, cryptic and hard to access. Below are some tips and suggestions for how to cultivate LP relationships, from someone who started with none of them, and how to eventually convert those relationships to $$ for your fund.

Disclaimer: *this is just one person's opinion and much of this is probably common sense. Also, the below focuses on LP relationship cultivation vs. how to run a fundraise process (building a deck, data room, LPA agreement, etc.). Still, I did identify some nuance to the LP game that may be helpful for folks who one day might have to navigate the fundraise grind.*

Getting Started

A challenge for most junior VCs is how to build initial relationships with people who who might actually invest in your fund.

I haven't found good "lists" (I know there's some on twitter, pitchbook but low signal IMO). So any actual bank of names you'd want to access doesn't really exist publicly... but hey it wouldn't be fun if you didn't have to hustle.

First, if you have a cheat code, use it. Objectively, and for better or worse (sometimes definitely worse) VCs are just privileged bunch. But

VC is also an industry where it makes sense to play to your strengths. Leverage those Harvard, Andover, Columbia, etc. networks, because why not (a caveat below in the "look out for yourself" section - always be the master of your own relationships).

For those of us embarking on this journey a bit behind the starting line (or at the starting line without a head start), the same logic applies. This is VC 101. Our industry is all about relationships, so use yours. Hustle, find wealthy people or people that work at family offices, fund-of-funds, etc. A key piece of advice: this is a <u>high signal game</u>. Think about how effective cold outreach is from startup to VC. It's even less effective as you go up the food chain from VC to LP.

Find the people in your network that will give you the most quality introduction to a potential LP. There is often no shortcut here. I've spent countless hours on LinkedIn identifying qualified LP targets and then an equal amount of time asking my professional friends and allies for warm introductions.

Also ask around… ask your friends, other people in finance, other investors, other people who orbit the $ universe. Lastly, once you do get a few good names and make a few good relationships, leverage them to find more opportunities (wealthy folks know wealthy folks, family office folks know family office folks, etc.). I was surprised how one relationship can turn into a vein of relationships.

Categorizing: I place LPs in three broad buckets:

1. <u>Too Big Too Raise From</u>: "Institutionals" → these are the big funding entities, endowments, large fund-of-funds, asset managers, etc. Unless you have a super deep pre-existing relationship with someone who can champion your fund,

spending a lot of time here is likely a waste of effort in the short-term but can be beneficial for longer-term goals (i.e. keeping a relationship warm across fund cycles).

a. First, if you're a fund who has these folks as LPs your partners have been cultivating these relationships for a long time. Best bet is to just be in the room and try to develop your own relationships with these folks by shining bright.

b. Second, if you are a new fund or a fund under a certain size (total AUM ~$100M) you are likely too small for these funds. It would be like hunting for a whale shark with a worm (bad analogy - whale sharks should never be fished, they are magical!).

c. Third, if your fund is just at the point where they are engaging with these giants, note that the process can take a long time (sometimes years and multiple fund cycles!). You're most likely going to tap your network and get connected to a junior person, which will just extend an already lengthy process. If you were able to generate this relationship for your fund, that's awesome, but you might not even be at the fund if and when it could come to fruition. Worth building those relationships though you never know.

2. Goldilocks: Family Offices / Smaller Fund-to-Funds, Corporations (although still a pain)

a. Depending on the size of your fundraise and how much you hope (or are expected) to bring in, I'd spend most of my time in this goldilocks zone. Family offices and smaller fund-to-funds (and sometimes corporates) can write sizable seven figure checks and can move much faster that institutionals. Also, these folks tend to be a bit more accessible and open to introductions.

b. Take advantage of the increased interest in VC from entities that historically don't focus on "alternative assets". Some family offices are just starting their consideration of venture investing, so you may seem like an exotic asset or a way for them to "diversify". Definitely keep that in mind as you engage these entities, especially those that aren't sophisticated in fund investing.

c. Be focused, try to back into what they are looking for → this is really difficult since many of these people don't tweet or publicly articulate their investment theses, but try to find if there's a focus on areas or subjects (diversity, crypto, sustainability, etc.)

3. <u>Anything Helps</u>: High Net Worth individuals (HNW), friends, family - won't move the needle but good network to have and good to put points on the board

a. These are the folks in your network who might be able to invest $50K and low six figure checks. Successful entrepreneurs, other VCs, wealthy family friends, etc. Not meant to move the needle but good to put points on the board and show your fund you are contributing. Also, these folks can usually point you in the direction of people interested in making similar sized investments and once in a while hopefully make a connection to a Goldilocks type person.

Maintaining and Cultivating Relationships

There's alternate strategies for engaging potential LPs after you make that initial contact / relationship. An obvious one is bringing them into deals directly. While funds typically prioritize existing LPs for any direct or SPV opportunities, it's still a chance to engage high priority potential investors. I wouldn't do this for a $50K check unless they can be a real value add to the company (and to your fund beyond the capital) but making the case to engage one or two new potential investors via direct investing opportunities can pay dividends.

Also flow of data and information is critical. As the sales cycle can be long and stretch over multiple months, make sure to keep on radars by sending relevant updates and successes (while not spamming). Recent investments, big company raises articles on relevant subjects that relate to your investment strategy. For example say you had a conversation about healthcare data regulation and how it pertains to your investment focus that is then supported by a WSJ article other prominent LPs who commit, etc. Staying relevant via communicating legitimate updates and data points is a great way to keep the relationship warm.

Peacetime vs. War time

Somewhat obvious point, but it can be a lot easier to develop relationships when you're not actively fundraising. In my experience it takes some of the pressure off the "sell / buy" dynamic. Anyone who is gearing up for a fundraise might want to pursue intros / develop relationships before you're in the heat of the fundraising cycle.

Buy vs. Sell

As one might know instinctively, fundraising exercises a totally different muscle vs. investing (I found that one of the great side benefits to fundraising is increased empathy for/from entrepreneurs) since you are fundamentally selling vs. buying. Knowing your product, your customer (potential LP), and your points of differentiation as a fund are critical first steps towards building successful relationships - in casual settings or during actual pitches. I would definitely make sure the message is honed before you go live with pitching / networking. Even though we do it every day in normal conversations, it personally took me a bit to get really good at pitching our fund for this audience.

Looking out for yourself

For those of us in the earlier stages of our career, and especially for those at funds that don't have a clear path to partnership, I'd encourage you to look out for yourself!

If you bring in these relationships, make sure to maintain and own them. Don't let yourself be cut out of communication channels, email chains, etc. Ok to hand them off to a partner, but make sure that any relationship between your fund and that LP evolves with you at the helm (or at least a co-pilot position).

Lastly, if you are fortunate enough to already have great LP relationships, be careful how you use them. If you are more junior and don't want to stay at a fund for 5 years you may want to think twice about spending this social / professional capital for a fund that you end up leaving. If those investors are investing because of you, you may only get one ask. Generally, I'd keep my Aces (and maybe even my Kings and Queens, to batter the analogy) in my hand unless I had a ton of conviction about my future at my current fund.

Day 2: **What do LPs look for in funds**

William Leonard - Valor Ventures
Meghan Hillery, Molly Cline - Coventure

Venture capital is truly a long game. VC is an incredibly illiquid asset class compared with other vehicles where LPs can park their capital. With the asset class so illiquid, venture investors need metrics to illustrate early performance across the fund's lifecycle. It takes a long time to determine the full performance of a VC fund, typically more than 10 years. When funds aren't fully realized, there are still numerous ways LPs can track metrics to assess fund performance.

At a high level, VC performance tends to be measured through 3 key metrics: TVPI, DPI, and IRR.

TVPI: Total Value Paid In Capital in plain terms measures the total value of the fund's holdings (realized and unrealized) divided by the capital that has been called by the fund or "paid in" by LPs. TVPI is a simple fund performance metric but it's key to remember that TVPI does NOT account for the time value of money. TVPI's are typically high when an investor has significant paper mark-ups on investments.

- **Quick TVPI example:** LPs have contributed $5M into a venture fund, the fund has distributed $250K back to LPs and the firm's general partners estimate the Net asset value of their holdings to be $4.5M

- Add the residual value of $4.5M and distributions ($250K) to calculate the total value of $4.75M

- Divide that number by the total paid in capital ($5M) to get a TVPI of .95x – meaning based on the current value of assets, LPs have lost 5% of their investment.

DPI: Distributions Paid in Capital in layman's terms measures how much money a VC fund has sent back to LPs divided by the amount of money the LP has paid into the fund. DPI is the metric that matters most to LPs, the higher the better. In the long run you're focused on the DPI of a fund, in the short term TVPI is the key metric to assess early fund performance.

- **Quick DPI example:** A fund has called $50M in capital, distributed $60M to LPs, and has a NAV of $70M – meaning the total value here is $130M ($70M+$60M)

- To calculate the DPI, you take $60M (distributions) / $50M (paid in capital), therefore the DPI = 1.2x

- If the DPI is greater than one, the fund has returned all of its paid in capital to LPs. In this case LPs have received back all of their paid in capital of $50M + 20%.

IRR: The Internal Rate of Return is an approximation of the rate of appreciation of the fund's assets. With IRR, this number represents theoretical gains and not true gains given the illiquidity of private stock. True fund IRR will be based on the actual flow of cash in and out of an LPs account.

In addition to these quantitative metrics, LPs also consider qualitative characteristics when evaluating a VC fund. Being in a capital raising role, there are questions that come up consistently throughout the diligence process aimed at getting to know the VC firm, the given firm's edge and how they think about the world. Please see examples of these qualitative aspects below. It's important to note that because these traits can be more subjective, an LP's preferences for these characteristics can vary, and not all LPs evaluate funds the same way.

- **Team & Culture:** Though it may sound basic this was one of the more important aspects to me when performing due diligence on a fund. I liked to see the following when looking a fund's team and culture: effort to cultivate diversity in multiple aspects, strong leadership team that has had no (or minimal) turnover, passion and commitment to the business, collaboration & idea sharing, constant focus on ways to improve and grow, constant desire to learn more & expand viewpoints, among many others. Ultimately, most institutional LPs are searching for funds they can partner with over multiple fund cycles. Being able to demonstrate team continuity and a strong firm culture is critical. LPs want to have trust that they are putting their money behind the right team to drive results.

- **Process:** Luck is certainly a part of success in investing, but LPs can't rely on a firm to generate consistent performance if they've just been lucky. It is important for a fund to be able to articulate how they look at investments and why it has made them successful. Ability to clearly communicate the underwriting process is important - LPs often found it helpful when a fund provided tangible examples of this process put into practice.

- **Source of Differentiation:** I always used to ask, "Why should I invest in you and not another firm just like you?" Having a unique perspective and/or clear source of differentiation from other funds is key. Funds have to be able to demonstrate how they are different from everyone else, and in turn, why it makes them better and how it has contributed to their success. Pro tip: saying that your network is better than anyone else's, and that's what makes you different / more successful, is not a source of differentiation.

- **Risk Management:** Venture investing, and any investing for that matter, is inherently risky, especially at the early stage. You should always keep in mind what could go wrong and the mechanisms you can put in place to avoid that. It's important for a firm to demonstrate clear ways they are managing risk when talking to LPs. At the end of the day, someone is trusting you with their money (it's someone's retirement plan, a scholarship for a student, etc.).

- **Value Add:** All VC firms will say they add value to their portfolio companies, but do they really? A metaphor I heard & liked when I was an LP was that in Buyout investing, you're taking the keys and putting yourself in the driver's seat. In VC investing, you're letting the founder drive the car, but you're in the passenger seat directing them where to go. Being in the passenger seat doesn't mean you're doing everything (remember: you're not the driver); rather, it means you're helping them out along the road trip (i.e. finding customers or new hires, making introductions, helping identify KPIs & ways to measure them, etc.). I'd recommend that firms track the ways they've helped their portfolio companies and be able to provide metrics when asked (i.e. made X introductions over the last year, placed X key hires in portfolio companies, etc.). Being able to point to numbers or examples when talking about your value-add capabilities will bring your hard work to life for an LP and show that you take your responsibility as the passenger seriously.

Day 3: **How to think about angel investing**

Andrew Rea - Founder @ Taxwire / Angel @ Loft Capital

Angel Investors are an important source of social, financial, and belief capital for early-stage startups. They get less press than founders and VCs, but they play a crucial role in supporting the startup ecosystem.

If you're going to invest in startups, you need to understand their role, motivation, operating styles, etc. I'll also discuss the merits of angel investing personally and how to get started.

Finally, I hope this will prompt more junior VCs to build relationships with angel investors. Collaborating with great angels is something a lot of junior VCs underinvest in.

Side note: These days, everyone in tech seems to be an angel investor, making it hard to speak broadly about this topic. For sake of brevity, I'm only referring to the highest-caliber angel investors in this piece.

Context on Me
Why should you listen to me?

Well, you definitely shouldn't just listen to me. This is data. This is my pov. There are folks smarter than me on Angel Investing. I recommend meeting them, reading their blogs, and studying their pov. Multiple perspectives and data points are the best path to forming your own judgment.

That said, I do know a few things about this topic.

- I've been in venture and startups for 5 years. At this point, I've worn all the major hats that someone in this ecosystem can – founder, operator, venture capitalist, and angel investor.

- I've seen fundraising from both sides of the table (founder vs VC/Angel).

- I've seen investing from both POVs – first as a junior VC. Second, as an angel investor.

- I've invested in ~20 startups across SPVs (that I've led) and personal checks.

All that to say, I have some level of experience and am not just some utter rando. If you want to know more about my background, you can skim this[32].

Angel Investors' Role in the Startup Ecosystem

Angel investing is a social, financial, and cultural game that keeps early-stage startup formation and funding dynamic.

Angel investing culture is one of the reasons San Francisco has long been the top place for early-stage startups. I'd argue it's one of the main edges SF has over other startup cities. The quality of a city's startup community is directly correlated with the depth and vitality of its angel investing ecosystem.

The common wisdom is that an angel's most important role is in investing in startups before most VCs can or will. This is partially

---

[32] https://andrewrea.xyz/

true, but I think the most important role these days is less money and more belief and social capital.

Belief and Social Capital

1. Angels are often the founder's first believer. That belief can be more impactful than the size of the check they are writing, especially for first-time founders or founders that are outsiders by background.

2. Angels use their social capital to help founders succeed. Most angels often have more social capital than financial capital. They have reputations, personal brands, networks, and expertise. Angels use their social capital to help entrepreneurs bootstrap their own. Angels help founders learn how to play the game. They leverage social capital to make fundraising, recruiting, and customer intros. They teach founders how to talk to other investors, etc.

Neither belief nor social capital are explicitly about financial capital. They are their own unique forms of capital and should be recognized as such.

First-time and/or "Outsider" Founders

Angels use their belief and social capital to help outsiders and/or inexperienced entrepreneurs break through.

The right angel taking a bet on a founder before it's obvious can be trajectory-changing. When you dig into the early fundraising journeys of many startups, you'll start to notice how common this is.

- Ron Conway is famous for doing this for dozens, maybe hundreds of companies.

- Naval has done this <u>for many companies</u>[33].

- Dan Gilbert (billionaire founder of Rocket Mortgage and the owner of the Cleveland Cavaliers) was the first investor in a my friend's first company based in Detroit. His investment led to my friend dropping out of school, subsequently getting the Thiel Fellowship, and raising from tier 1 investors.

- Another friend went from a complete Silicon Valley outsider to raising millions from respected angels and VCs due to meeting and convincing <u>Gokul Rajaram</u>[34] to invest.

- My friend <u>Julian Weisser</u>[35] was one of the first checks into a company founded by a then 18-year-old. His early investment and subsequent introductions lead to him raising millions while still living with his parents.

Momentum Capital

Related to the last point, good angels are often instrumental in helping an early startup get fundraising momentum.

My friend Julian calls this momentum capital[36]. As an example, data startup Freshpaint[37] raised over $700K from introductions made by an investor that wrote a $5K check[38].

---

[33] https://spearhead.co/shadow
[34] https://www.linkedin.com/in/gokulrajaram1/
[35] https://www.linkedin.com/in/julianweisser/
[36] https://twitter.com/julianweisser/status/1569446737328369667
[37] https://www.freshpaint.io/blog/anatomy-of-a-seed-round-during-covid-19
[38] https://twitter.com/julianweisser/status/1554221525003165696

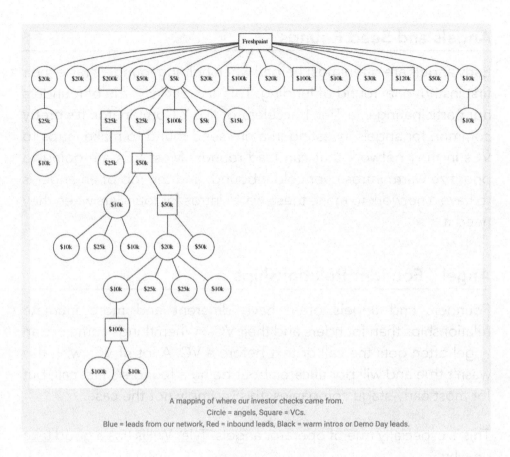

A mapping of where our investor checks came from.
Circle = angels, Square = VCs.
Blue = leads from our network, Red = inbound leads, Black = warm intros or Demo Day leads.

One of my very first angel investments was into a startup called Steady Capital[39]. I was lucky and nervous to invest, since my check size was so small. At the time, most of my network was limited to operator angels. Despite that, I made ~10 introductions that lead to ~$500k in other angels coming into the pre-seed. It all happened in about a week or so.

Momentum compounds in fundraising and angels can be a key driver in helping startups get it.

---

[39] https://www.steady.capital/

Angels and Seed Rounds

Early angels are often most helpful when helping founders raise their first institutional round of funding. This is especially true of founders not participating in a Tier 1 accelerator like Y Combinator. It's pretty common for angels investing in a pre-seed round to make intros to VCs in their network that can lead rounds. Most VCs are going to prioritize warm intros over cold inbound, and the job of an angel is to have a network to make these warm intros for founders when they need it.

Angel / Founder Relationships

Founders and angels often have different and more intimate relationships than founders and their VCs. When things come up, an angel often gets the call or text before a VC. A lot of VCs wish this wasn't true and will pontificate about being a founder's first call, but for most early-stage companies, this is simply not the case.

This is especially true of operator angels. Tyler Willis has a good take on why[40]:

It's hard to describe the thousands of operator angels with generalities that apply to all of us, but there are a few common traits:

- *We generally have friendlier and less structured relationships with founders, chiefly because we're still in the trenches working on our startups while we're investing and are at a more similar career stage to the founders starting new companies.*

---

[40] https://tyler.is/posts/what-operator-angels-are-and-why-they-are-suddenly-everywhere/

- *Founders look to us for more actionable and relevant advice on dealing with challenges, because we've often seen the same issues recently in our own companies.*

- *We are more likely to invest in companies early because we know the people starting these companies well (they are often our friends and peers) and we can be quicker to spot important emerging trends.*

It's possible but less probable for a VC to have this relationship with a founder, especially if you're the lead investor and/or sit on the board and have consequential decision making power on things like follow-on investments or compensation, as examples

There are many more things that could be said about angel investors and the role they play, but I think these are a few of the more relevant ones to junior investors. I also think some of these are less discussed in broader startup media.

Why do people Angel Invest

Understanding the nuances of why people angel invest is helpful. Financial returns are often just one of several motivators.

- **Social Capital & Status** – Silicon Valley runs on social capital and status. Those that are able to break through the barriers and make introductions can go far fast.

- **Career Goals** – Many start angel investing because they have the aspiration of becoming a venture capitalist and getting a job at a fund. I have several friends that broke into venture this way.

- **Track Record** – Many angels are trying to build their personal investing track record so that they can go raise their own fund someday.

- **Learning** – Meeting and learning directly from founders about markets, products, and companies is an incredible function for learning. It's probably one of the reasons you became a VC. There is information and context you get being on a founder's investor update that you'll never get from reading their Techcrunch fundraising announcement.

- **Altruism / Giving Back** – Many former founders invest to give back and pay it forward to the next generation. Some invest because they see it as a way to express a worldview (e.g. many climate tech angels).

- **Friendship** – Some invest to express belief and participate in their friend's journey. Little is as rewarding as helping someone you love get their company off the ground.

- **Financial Returns** – The most obvious and hardest to achieve, but a lot of folks do see angel investing as a way to get rich and become the next Jason Calacanis.

Working with Angels for Junior VCs

Build Relationships

I'm always surprised by how few junior VCs attempt to build relationships with angel investors. I'm biased but I believe building relationships with a few high-quality angels can be a meaningful edge in sourcing and diligencing investments.

A strategy I'd recommend is building relationships with emerging angels. Don't try to become friends with Elad Gil. He already has a great network. Also, your partners probably already have relationships with established folks like him. Rather, your energy will be better spent trying to find and work with the next Elad Gil.

If you do decide to build relationships with angels, make sure you're actually helpful. A lot of VCs will reach out to me and try to extract deal flow without building a relationship or providing tangible value that would make me want to introduce them to founders in the first place. It's a bad look and almost a guarantee that they will never see a deal from me.

Treat Founder Intros Thoughtfully

No VC is going to invest in every deal I or any other angel sends them. In some cases, they won't even take the meeting. That's okay.

However, you should do your best to be thoughtful regardless of whether or not you pass.

If you don't want to take the meeting, pass quickly and thoughtfully. Even better, share the context on why you're passing. It helps angels filter for what you like and what kind of deals to send you.

If you do take the meeting, show up prepared and treat the founder with respect. If you pass, do it quickly and respectfully. This really should apply to every meeting you take with founders. I can guarantee that if you treat a founder I introduced you to poorly, I'll hear about it and that you will never see another deal from me.

Angel Profiles

Some angel profiles worth knowing for junior VCs.

Operator Angels

Folks that actively invest and get lots of deal flow. Either from their position as an operator, founder, or another leverageable position in the ecosystem.

Examples:

- Ayokunle Omojola[41] gets great deal flow in fintech and healthcare because he's a subject matter expert on both topics, and he has clout from being early Cash App.

- James Beshara[42] made his early angel investments from his position as a YC founder and having a customer base that included companies like Gusto.

- Myself. I got started by leveraging my position at On Deck and Party Round (now Capital). My job was literally building products for founders and other investors. That got me insight and access to deals before a lot of others did.

Future Professional Investors

Someone with aspirations of raising a fund, a young operator chasing a job in venture, an angel trying to professionalize, etc. These folks are worth noting because they take investing more seriously and tend to be quite active in scouting deals.

---

[41] https://www.linkedin.com/in/omojola/
[42] https://jjbeshara.com/about/

Alumni Networks

The most famous company alumni network is the PayPal mafia, but you'll find these networks all over tech. The level of entrepreneurial activity from alums can vary significantly and doesn't always track to the size of exit or valuation. For example, product hunt is a relatively small company that achieved a small exit. However, that alumni network has gone on to do incredible things.

Brands

Folks with big followings on Twitter, podcasts, blogs, etc. These folks were often the types of people that raised rolling funds in 2021. Examples would include Ben Zises[43], Paige Finn Doherty[44], and Meagan Loyst[45].

Should you Angel Invest?

Nuances for VCs

For junior VCs, navigating angel investing can be tricky.

First, it's essential to ensure that your firm allows it and that there are no conflicts of interest. Every firm has its own policy, and the decision to invest as a junior VC will depend on your specific situation.

If your firm allows it, there are real benefits to building your own portfolio, particularly if you plan to be a long-term investor. As a junior VC, it can be difficult to get attribution for deals you've worked on, and your track record is critical for advancing your venture career.

---

[43] https://twitter.com/bzises?ref_src=twsrc%5Egoogle%7Ctwcamp%5Eserp%7Ctwgr%5Eauthor

[44] https://twitter.com/paigefinnn

[45] https://twitter.com/meaganloyst

Angel investing can be a way to supplement your portfolio and demonstrate your ability to pick and get access to great companies.

If your firm focuses on specific themes or sectors, angel investing can be an avenue to invest in other categories that interest you. For example, if you work for a deep tech fund but also have an affinity for CPG brands, angel investing is a great avenue to explore that.

Accredited Investor Qualifications

To be an angel investor, you have to be an <u>accredited investor</u>[46].

The main qualifications for an individual to be considered an accredited investor are:

- **Net Worth** – Having a net worth exceeding $1 million, either individually or jointly with a spouse, excluding the value of your primary residence

- **Annual Income** – Earning at least $200,000 individually or $300,000 jointly with a spouse for the past two years, with the expectation of maintaining the same income level in the current year.

There are some additional categories of accredited investor that are worth noting:

- **Entities** – Entities such as any bank, broker-dealer or registered investment adviser registered with the SEC, state securities commission or relying upon an exemption.

---

[46] https://www.investopedia.com/terms/a/accreditedinvestor.asp

- **Professional Certifications** – Individuals holding in good standing certain professional designations, such as the Series 65, 7, and 82.

- **Knowledgeable Employees** – An executive officer, director, general partner or person serving in a similar capacity of a private fund. Additionally, a non-clerical or administrative employee who participates in the investment activities of the private fund.

What does this most likely mean for you?

- If you make, $200k and are single, you're probably good.

- If you work at a fund, there's a good chance that you can legally invest in your fund as an LP or potentially into specific deals with your personal capital.

If you can't do either of the above, there's a side door through the Series 65 (the easiest of the professional certifications to attain) that lets you become accredited. The challenging part is getting a place to sponsor your license (typically an RIA). I went through this process a few years ago. You can read more about it here[47].

Note: None of the above is financial or investment advice. Do your own research and talk to an attorney or financial advisor about your situation.

Tips for Actually Writing Your Own Checks

Sakib asked me to share more tactical tips on how to actually angel invest. How to invest is an inherently broad and subjective topic. As I said earlier, you get multiple POVs on topics like this and then trust your own judgment.

---

[47] https://andrewrea.substack.com/p/becoming-an-accredited-investor-with

What I will do is share the lessons I've learned so far. I'll also link a few of my favorite resources for folks that are just getting started.

What I've learvned so far

In no particular order:

- **Invest the same check size every time:** It keeps things simple for you and you don't have to explain your check size to founders on each deal.

- **Double down on winners:** If you have a great company and the access + leverage to build more ownership, do it.

- **Don't invest for status:** It was high status to invest in crypto startups in 2021, but it's not today. Writing a check because a company or sector is high status is a bad long-term investment decision. Your heart is not in the right place, and you'll end up regretting the decision.

- **If it doesn't make sense, don't do the deal:** It doesn't matter if a16z or Sequoia is leading the round. Trust your judgment. Don't back a business you don't understand.

- **Know the game you're playing:** Not everyone is playing the same game. Angels are playing a very different game than a mega fund.

- **Writing checks is the best way to learn:** You'll learn way more by having skin in the game than you will by reading alone or helping someone else invest.

- **Backing your friends is always worth it:** In fact, you'll regret not doing it. Find a way to write the check.

- **Play the long game:** This is one of the most illiquid asset classes in the world. It's also a very cyclical industry. Missing a platform shift can cost you a generation of returns. Only play this game if you are in it for the long haul.

- **Put in the reps:** My judgment and pattern matching is 10x better today than it was 2 years ago. And in 10 years I'll probably be embarrassed by the current version of myself. The real rewards come from letting knowledge, capital, and relationships compound.

- **Always respond to investor updates:** It's easy to do, but you'd be surprised by how few investors do it. If you've ever been on the other side, you know how much effort can go into those.

- **Get on a texting basis as fast as possible:** Deals get done via message. Texting is also much more intimate to most people than email. If you want to build relationships and get things done, share your number liberally and be as responsive as possible.

- **Pass thoughtfully:** Fundraising is really hard. Being thoughtful about a pass goes a long way.

- **Be kind.** Life is too short to do anything else, and you'd be surprised how rude many investors are.

- **Try to help everyone:** It won't always be possible, but go into every meeting with another founder or investor thinking of how you can help this person. Don't just ask how you can help. Proactively suggest ways that you can help.

- **Don't unnecessarily gatekeep:** If you think two people should meet, don't think about what it's in it for you. Trust your instincts and make the intro.

- **Invest in what you understand:** Invest in spaces you have an edge in. Do the work to gain an edge as new categories emerge. Don't start investing in a new market or sector without doing the work to understand what you're doing.

- **Stay curious and open-minded:** Strong opinions loosely held is a trite thing to talk about, but this industry can humble you fast if you don't keep an open mind.

- **Take everyone default seriously:** You never know what someone else will become. What's more, you were once an outsider too. Help people, and treat them with dignity and respect.

Additional reading:

- What are Operator Angels – Tyler Willis[48]

- Angel Investing Start Guide – Sam Huleatt[49]

- How to be an Angel Investor – Paul Graham[50]

- How to be an Angel Investor pt 2. – Venture Hacks / Naval[51]

- How to be an Angel Investor pt. 1 – Naval[52]

- How to be an Angel Investor pt. 2 – Naval[53]

---

[48] https://tyler.is/posts/what-operator-angels-are-and-why-they-are-suddenly-everywhere/
[49] https://samhuleatt.com/resources/angel-investing-start-guide
[50] http://www.paulgraham.com/angelinvesting.html/
[51] https://venturehacks.com/angel/
[52] https://nav.al/angel-1/
[53] https://nav.al/angel-2/

- Investing Secrets – Naval[54]

- Fred Wilson on Investing in web 2.0 (old transcription from a 2009 interview)[55]

- Peter Pan and Neverland VC Returns – Bullflight Capital[56]

- The Social Subsidy of Angel Investing – Alex Danco[57]

- **Investing in Public:** Non-Obvious Lessons from 100+ Angel Investments – Tod Sacerdotti[58]

- How to Break into Startup Investing – Erik Torenberg[59]

- Elad Gil's blog[60]

- Jerry Neuman's blog[61]

Reach out

I truly hope this helps. Congrats on breaking into venture. It's a tough job to get. The ecosystem needs more investors that do good work and treat founders well.

If I can ever help or you'd like to connect, please reach out.

---

[54] https://www.navalmanack.com/secret-sections/investing/
[55] https://www.howardlindzon.com/p/way-back-machinewhat-feel-like-investing-web-2009-chat-fred-wilson/
[56] https://bullfight.substack.com/p/peter-pan-and-neverland-vc-returns/
[57] https://alexdanco.com/2019/11/27/the-social-subsidy-of-angel-investing/
[58] https://alexdanco.com/2019/11/27/the-social-subsidy-of-angel-investing/
[59] https://eriktorenberg.substack.com/p/how-to-break-into-startup-investing/
[60] https://blog.eladgil.com/p/7-types-of-angel-investors-what-is
[61] http://reactionwheel.net/

Day 4: **Productizing the job - what is the VC tech stack?**

Jack McClelland – Afore Capital
Vaneezeh Siddiqui – Thomson Reuters Ventures

Venture can feel like an information overload when you first start. Especially as a junior on the team, you're jumping between founder calls, thesis research, ecosystem events, relationship building, portfolio company projects, and fund activities. At the end of the day, your job is to find stellar companies and invest in them, and you want to give yourself the time to learn the art of investing. This section of the book explains how to leverage software to automate your workflows so that you can get more done, free up time for strategic work, and regain control of your to-do list.

How Do You Choose What to Include in Your Tech Stack?

At an emerging fund, youmay have more flexibility with the types of tools that can be used because there's a level of scrappiness that comes with smaller teams. At a corporate venture fund, other factors need to be considered, such as security, implementation feasibility, and compatibility with existing systems. Some factors that will affect what your tech stack looks like include the size of your team, your day to day activities, the number of portfolio companies your fund supports, financial resource constraints, compliance systems, the volume of deals you evaluate, and the stages of your investment process.

Before you set up anything new, assess how you and your team work best. Reflect on the daily tasks that are repetitive or time consuming. It's easier to make a choice about what software to try once you know the process flow you're trying to imitate. For example, if you're choosing your CRM, ask: what stages of the investment process should be tracked? ? Would it be helpful to link all email communications to specific deals if your team is large? A trap I had fallen into was thinking that more tech was better, when in practice it made more sense to integrate with the tools we were already using -- something to be mindful of.

How should I use this guide within a guide?

The below table buckets our recommended tech stack based on a VCs day to day tasks. While not all of these are tried and tested, this should serve as a good starting point. *VCStack.io* might also be a good first resource to explore since they have a huge database of categorized tools.

Category	Apps/Tools "all links in bit.ly/ YoungVCBookLinks"
CRM	Airtable: Database infrastructure that connects well to automation tools like Zapier or GMass. Streak: A clean Gmail Chrome extension with a CRM built for venture work, but only useful if your team is using GSuite. Affinity: The most commonly used CRM built specifically for VC. The software focuses on focus of the platform is relationship intelligence and collaborative deal management. Dialllog: Project based CRM built specifically for VC funds and the investor workflow. Clay: AI powered personal CRM that has interesting features like notifying when a contact's Twitter bio has changed,

Category	Apps/Tools "all links in bit.ly/YoungVCBookLinks"
Research	Volv: Summarizes the news into 9 second chunks and allows you to personalize your news feed. Glimpse: Free Chrome extension to see search volume in Google Trends, set alerts, and build topic maps. Open VC: A huge database of all the VC funds with the option to filter through entries. Product Hunt: Find the newest trending software products (some of the tools on this list have had PH launches!) Harmonic: A data engine tracking startups, with the option to create detailed filters and get notified on what you're tracking via their API. Crunchbase: Comprehensive database of companies at all stages. Pitchbook: Popular source for data and insights into market trends.

Category	Apps/Tools "all links in bit.ly/YoungVCBookLinks"
Communication	<u>Slack</u>: Well known for internal team communications, but also has great integration with tools like Zapier (ex: automatically create a Slack channel for a deal). <u>GMass:</u> Mass email organization and can be used to send things like portfolio updates or cold emails. <u>Superhuman</u>: One of the most talked about email clients that makes going through emails faster. This is also a pricier software. <u>Notion</u>: Useful for internal team documentation and task tracking. I've also used this to track progress on professional goals for performance reviews. manager <u>Bridge</u>: A tool to manage, keep track of, and send intros. <u>Loom</u>: A screen and video recording tool that's useful for sending internal team updates or quick explanations to save on meeting time.

Category	Apps/Tools "all links in bit.ly/YoungVCBookLinks"
Scheduling	<u>Calendly</u>: The source of many Twitter debates, but has all the key features of a scheduling tool . <u>Amie</u>: A startup building a new way to be productive. The ability to drag and drop to do list items into your calendar is my favourite feature. <u>Cron</u>: Voted productivity app of the year on Product Hunt with great team features and a visually appealing interface.

A few categories that are not included here, but may be important to consider depending on your role at the fund:

- LP Reporting

- Community

- Backend: Fund Infrastructure, Cap-table Management *(ex: Carta, AngelList)*

- Platform: Portfolio Perks, Job Boards *(ex: Cabal, Visible, Pallet)*

In addition to the tactical piece, here are some suggestions for practical functions as well.

Sourcing – increasing top of funnel opportunities:

Scraping for founders or looking for early-signal data is perhaps the most common and obvious tooling that we have seen firms prioritize. It can vary from simple LinkedIn or professional network / broader webs scraping, along with automating outreach or outreach processes (e.g. drafting a customized email) in cases that make sense.

Many firms attempt to do it in-house, with more internal resources to build and maintain (often the hard part) their own tool, while many others will buy tools like Harmony, Pitchbook, tryspecter.com, etc. where the disadvantage is that competing funds may have similar data. Regardless of the path your firm takes, it may make sense to consider championing the process e.g. if your fund does not have the resources to build in-house, simply doing research and figuring out the right vendor for your firm may be considered a high-value activity.

Picking – evaluating and prioritizing leads

Moving down the funnel, it may makes sense to automate certain evaluation criteria as well. It can be suggestions i.e. scoring, or full decision-making, for example, discounting a company that has already raised ~$10M+ in equity if you are a pre-seed fund. One fund has built an AI / decision-making engine that creates pros and cons for a company and helps the investor figure out what they should be spending time on.

Diligence - identifying what to look for and assisting with data

Moving even further down the funnel, once you have decided that a certain investment is worth spending time on, many firms are automating what was historically known as 'the checklist'. People have used things like ChatGPT to automate writing or Consumer Edge to utilize data at a granular level, and at a higher level, some firms have tracked overall market dynamics to find "rising tides" so to speak.[62]

Automating intros during a live process and after investment - a huge part of a VC's job is to introduce founders / investors to each other; engineers can build mail merge tools or ones similar to intros or bridge. There are full stack solutions like cabal and pinched.io that can track and present full social graphs in a digestible manner.

General workflow automation - this covers numerous functions, but some specific examples could be pulling founder information from cold inbound forms and piping this into a VC's CRM for example. Firms have previously used tools like Zapier, but there are a number of bespoke solutions you can build from the ground-up.

LP-side work - this could involve building an LP portal on a VC's website or interpreting data from portfolio companies to help automate LP reporting. Standardmetrics.io is a popular platform for this function.

There's room to play around with what's on the market and make adjustments to fit your specific use case. Investors are always coming up with novel methods to augment their tech stack or add value to founders in a differentiated way, and many are kept as state secrets.

---

[62] https://base10.vc/research/ and https://www.consumer-edge.com/

If you're technically inclined or curious about what is possible, here are a few sources to explore:

- 776 sends out auto generated "Founder Recap emails"[63] that show how they've supported their port-co founders using an OS they've built

- Yohei at Untapped VC[64] has great threads on building in public as he experiments with use cases of GPT, Dall-e, and other new tech for venture tasks

- As a data nerd, I (Vaneezeh) love this piece on using exploratory data analysis[65] to supercharge sourcing with Harmonic and Python, written by Aya Spencer at Kapor Capital

VC tomorrow will look very different from today. There are some funds that are already beginning to heavily introduce technology into their day-to-day workflow and portfolio support. Although there are many ways to achieve success in VC, with or without internal tooling, being data-driven could be a strong source of advantage and a great fundraising point to market to limited partners (LPs) – especially if you can become the internal champion for such functions at your firm.

---

[63] https://twitter.com/alexisohanian/status/1551344206509129729

[64] https://twitter.com/yoheinakajima/status/1561367119454908416?s=20&t=Ohwq2i zPkUQqOkrHOKFFSA

[65] https://ayacancode.medium.com/how-to-leverage-python-harmonic-to-supercharge-your-sourcing-7547e01fd33f

Day 5: **What are some exit opportunities from a career in venture?**

Aman Kandola - Formerly at Bessemer Venture Partners

There are many potential subsequent career paths for a VC associate, but the most common choices tend to be either staying in venture or transitioning into an operating role. That seems reductive, but even just navigating those two basic choices can be daunting because both of these career paths are dynamic, idiosyncratic, and progression is not necessarily linear. Making career decisions is also something that is highly personal so any advice has to be taken with a grain of salt. I'd also recommend <u>reading this post by Tim Urban</u>[66] that I and many of my friends have found helpful in thinking through their careers. In my opinion, the two most important pieces of advice I've received on making career choices is recognizing that careers are long and minimizing regret. Careers span multiple decades and even just a few years is a lifetime in tech so it's important to avoid too much attachment to the financial and status gain from quick progression along a single path if you aren't yet sure it's what you want to be doing because it gets harder to make significant career changes later on (partly because you won't want to yourself and partly because of bias in hiring practices) and instead it's better to try all of the things you think you might want to do and then settle with conviction on the path you find most exciting.

---

[66] https://waitbutwhy.com/2018/04/picking-career.html

The Career VC Path

If you somehow already know that VC is what you want to be doing forever, then your goal is likely to end up as a GP at a fund. It's hard to be too prescriptive given the differences in fund structure, but the first thing to do would be to determine if there is a path up at your current fund. In some funds, associate-level positions are intended to be a stepping stone to higher levels within the fund, but in other funds, the ladder starts higher up and associates are generally expected to cycle through after a few years. If you have a path up, then you can determine whether or not this is the fund you want to invest the energy into moving up at, or if you'd be better served somewhere else. Aside from the typical factors to consider for all kinds of jobs (workplace culture, the brand, etc.), the factors specific to VC that you'll want to figure out are:

- What are the fund economics (how is carry split)?

- Are there obvious expansion vectors for the fund? For example, if the fund does not currently have a practice in a specific industry vertical or a geographic area that you might be considered an expert in (and the fund has an interest in developing this practice), you might have a much easier time gaining leverage than if you work at a fund that already has high coverage.

- Does the fund have a history of developing talent? Some funds prefer to hire experienced operators as partners or may not be expanding the fund size at all, others are constantly working to retain and develop talent.

- What is the fund's investment philosophy? Are some industries off-limits? Are they looking to be active or passive investors? What stages do they invest in?

- What is the fund's investment process? Are deals referral-driven or is there a sourcing-heavy culture? What does the diligence process look like? Are investments decided by committees, individual partners, or senior management only?

It's important to think through all of those things because once you start building a portfolio at a fund it can become messy to leave. If you can't find a fund that matches what you're looking for, you can always start your own!

The Operating Path

When I was considering my options after two years at Bessemer Venture Partners, I was set on pursuing an operating role. There were three types of roles I was exploring: starting a company, joining in a strategy or operations role at a later stage startup (Series C+) or joining as a generalist at an early stage startup (ideally post PMF).

1. **Starting a Company** - Some things that are really hard for most founders are really easy for VC Associates. Raising money should be pretty straightforward - you have an investor network and you've seen countless investment pitches. You might also be able to pitch your fund on an EIR role - the fund provides you with some initial support (e.g. capital in the form of an investment or a salary, an office, people to bounce ideas off) in exchange for continuing to use you in a limited capacity as an Associate. This is pretty ideal when you're still exploring ideas, but the pitfall is getting too comfortable, trying to over-optimize your initial approach, and delaying the actual building and selling for longer than you should. You also likely already have a great founder network - these are all people that have gone through this experience already

and can serve as a great resource for you when dealing with the initial struggles of getting started.

2. **Strategy, Business Operations, Finance** - If you have no prior operating experience, these are likely the roles you'll find yourself best positioned for. Your primary assets coming out of investing are financial modeling, business context, and analysis from first principles. Financial modeling is an obvious one - someone has to build these models for every startup and if you've done enough of this as an Associate and enjoyed it enough, then you would excel in a finance role at a startup. Most startups don't need a dedicated finance headcount until Series C. Business context is a loose term, but what I'm referring to is your general awareness of what different functions exist in a company, what they are working towards in theory, how they relate to each other, the market context of the company, and the strategic levers for the business. As an investor, you pick apart a company's operational metrics all the time - you know exactly what a marketing team focuses on, what a sales team focuses on, what good vs. bad pricing looks like, etc. When combined with your ability to approach a problem using first principles, you can find yourself impactful in any conversation in the business despite a lack of prior operating experience. Strategy and Business Operations roles tend to be the best-suited for honing these skills and applying them in practice.

3. **Generalist** - If you have no idea what you want to do at a startup, but you just want to try it out and are willing to hustle, then find a great early-stage team doing something you're excited about, and convince them to make a role for you. Great founders are always looking to bring on great talent, even if they don't know what they'll need you for. Lucky for them, you

should be great at figuring out what any given startup should be executing on so you can identify the areas of greatest opportunity for the team given their current composition, craft a role for yourself executing on those opportunities, and then sell the founder on your ability to execute while managing yourself so you create no additional overhead for anyone else on the team. If you join early enough, you'll get a chance to experience a taste of every function and then you can eventually narrow in on the ones you enjoy the most. This was what I ultimately ended up going with - I joined Courier as the first business hire just after the Series A and it's been an amazing journey so far.

As far as recruiting for an operating role, great startups are always looking for great talent and founders generally take candidate recommendations from their investors so I wouldn't be afraid to leverage your network for introductions to their portfolios and using that as an opportunity to learn more about what roles are available. When I was still in VC, I often felt that I had no transferable skills to operating, but I've been surprised fairly often by how wrong I was - thinking like an investor is a useful skill itself in some operating environments.

Ultimately, the general career advice you've probably heard from other folks is always relevant - work with people you love working with and find a job that gives you enough flexibility to enjoy your life (this includes having free time!). The rest is just details.

Feel free to reach out to me directly if you want to chat about my experience or if you're looking for a sounding board!

Glossary

Courtesy of Confluence.vc

** Denotes deeper dives available on on select terms/concepts on the supplemental links document, type in **bit.ly/YoungVCBookLinks** (case sensitive) on your browser.*

409A Valuation: A 409a valuation is an estimate of the fair market value of a company's common stock. This valuation is established by an independent third party.

ARPU: ARPU is a metric used by companies to measure the average revenue generated by each of their customers. This figure is calculated by dividing total revenue by the number of active customers in a given period of time.*

AOV: The average order value (AOV) is a metric used by companies to measure the average value of each order that is placed on their website. This figure is calculated by dividing total revenue by the number of orders placed in a given period of time.

ARRG (Annual Recurring Revenue to Growth) Ratio: The ARRG (Annual Recurring Revenue to Growth) Ratio is a metric used by companies to measure the rate of growth of their annual recurring revenue. This figure is calculated by dividing the annual recurring revenue by the ARR growth rate over a period of time (usually a year).

Accelerator: An accelerator is a business incubator that provides funding, mentorship, and other resources to early-stage companies.

These organizations are typically focused on helping startups grow their businesses and achieve profitability.*

Accredited Investor: An accredited investor is a person or entity who has been granted special status by the Securities and Exchange Commission (SEC) due to their wealth or experience in the investment field. These investors are allowed to invest in high-risk securities that are not available to the general public.*

Allocation: Allocation is another term for the amount of capital an investor can contribute to a given financing round.

Anchor Investor: An anchor investor is the first check to commit to a given funding round. For startups, an anchor investor is the first fund that commits; for funds, it is the first limited partner to commit. This investor's participation gives other investors confidence that the startup is worth investing in, and can help persuade them to contribute to the round as well.

ARR (Annual Recurring Revenue): The ARR (annual recurring revenue) metric is used by companies to measure the amount of revenue that is generated on an annual basis from their customers. This figure is calculated by dividing the total revenue by the number of active customers in a given period of time.*

Angel Investor: An angel investor is an individual or organization that provides funding and other resources to early-stage startups. These investors are typically motivated by the potential for high returns, and are willing to take on greater risk in order to achieve them.*

Anti-Dilution Provision: An anti-dilution clause is a contractual provision that helps protect a company's shareholders from the dilutive effects of future rounds of financing. This clause ensures that the percentage of ownership held by each shareholder remains unchanged, even if the company raises more money at a lower valuation than the last round.

Blended Preferences: Blended preferences occur when an investor has a mix of preferred and common shares in the company. The preference means that the holder gets their money back first and also gets dividends or other distributions before the common shareholders.

Bootstrapping: This is when a company is self-funding its growth. This means that the startup is not reliant on outside investors to finance its operations, but is instead using its own revenue to finance its expansion. Bootstrapping can be a risky strategy, but it can also help a company avoid giving away too much equity to early investors.

Bridge Loan: A bridge loan is a short-term loan that is used to finance the gap between two rounds of financing. This loan is typically used to keep a company's operations running until it can secure more permanent funding. Bridge loans are typically either flat or down rounds.*

Burn Rate: The burn rate is a metric used by startups to measure the rate of expenditure on their operations. This figure is calculated by dividing the total amount of money that has been spent by the company in a given period of time by the average monthly burn rate.*

Capital Call: A capital call is a request by a fund for its limited partners to contribute more money to the fund. This call is made whenever the fund invests into new companies and needs to deploy capital.

Limited partners are usually contractually obligated to commit this capital under the limited partner agreement.

Cap Table: A cap table is a document that lists all of the shareholders in a company and their respective ownership stakes. This document is used by venture capitalists to track the ownership of a company and to determine the amount of capital that has been invested into it.*

Carried Interest ('carry'): A carried interest is a share of the profits that is earned by a venture capitalist as compensation for their services. This profit share is usually in addition to the capital that has been invested by the venture capitalist. Carried interest is generally only awarded to those investors who have achieved exceptional returns on their investments.

Cash-on-Cash Return (aka Multiple on Invested Capital or 'MOIC'): Cash-on-cash return (COCR) is the annual cash flow that an investor receives from their investment, divided by the amount of money invested. In venture capital, cash-on-cash is usually calculated at the end of a fund lifecycle. It is used as a lagging indicator to show how well the fund deployed capital, and it is used as marketing material to help the general partners pitch limited partners to raise their next fund.*

Churn: Churn rate is the percentage of customers that leave over a given period. Note you can talk about churn in terms of logos(customers) or revenue lost/upsold (net dollar retention)

Clawback: A clawback is a provision that allows limited partners to reclaim any carried interest paid during the life of the fund in order to normalize the final carry amount. This provision protects LPs from paying carried interest on one investment then incurring losses on the rest of their portfolio.*

Come Along Rights (aka Drag Along rights): Come along rights are a contractual provision that gives investors the right to join in on any future investment rounds. It may also mean that minority shareholders are forced to sell ('dragged along') when majority shareholders decide to sell their portion, unless agreed otherwise.

Common Stock: Common stock is a type of equity that represents ownership in a company. This type of stock typically has voting rights and entitles the holder to receive dividends from the company. Common stockholders are below preferred stockholders in the equity, and they are only paid after all preferred shareholders are compensated.*

Control Rights: Control rights are the rights that shareholders have to participate in the management of a company. These rights allow shareholders to vote on important company decisions, such as the election of directors or the sale of the company. Control rights also give shareholders the ability to veto certain actions that may be taken by the company's management.

Convertible Note: Convertible notes are a type of debt that can be converted into equity in a company. This type of debt usually has a lower interest rate than regular debt and allows the holder to purchase shares in the company at a discount.*

Corporate Venture Capital ('CVCs'): Corporate venture capital funds use corporate funds to invest into startups. These funds come off of the corporate balance sheet, and investment decisions are based on corporate strategy more than pure financial returns, although there are a few exceptions.

Covenant: A covenant is a contractual provision that primarily limits the amount of debt that a company can incur, or other restrictions that are agreed between two parties. This provision helps to protect the interests of lenders by ensuring that the company does not take on too much debt. Debt covenants are usually found in loan agreements and can include things such as the maximum amount of debt, the interest rate, and the maturity date.*

Cumulative Dividend: Cumulative dividends are a type of dividend that is paid to shareholders who have held their shares for a certain period of time. This dividend accumulates over time and is paid out in addition to the regular dividend payments. Cumulative dividends are usually only paid to those shareholders who are in good standing with the company.

Cutback Rights: Cutback rights are a contractual provision that gives investors the right to sell their shares back to the company at a predetermined price. This provision allows investors to sell their shares back to the company in order to protect their investment in case of a down round.

Demand Registration Rights: Demand registration rights are a contractual provision that gives investors the right to demand that their shares be registered with the SEC. This provision allows investors to sell their shares publicly if they choose to do so.

Dilution: Dilution in venture capital is the process of issuing new shares in a company which reduces the value of each existing share. This occurs when a company raises capital by issuing new shares, and can be caused by either a new investor coming into the company or by the conversion of debt to equity. Dilution can also occur when a company issues stock options to its employees (if it is not coming from a previously existing option pool).

Down Round: A down round is a funding round in which a company raises less money than it did in its previous round. This can be due to a number of factors, such as a decrease in the company's valuation or a decline in the market conditions. Down rounds are often seen as a sign of weakness and can be difficult for companies to overcome.

Drag-Along Rights: same as Come Along rights above

Due Diligence: Due diligence in venture capital is a process through which a company evaluates a potential investment. This process includes a review of the company's financials, as well as its business and operating plans. Due diligence is used to assess the risks and potential returns associated with investing in a company.*

Exit Velocity: Exit velocity is the rate at which a company is able to exit from its investments. This term is used primarily in venture capital and is used to measure the liquidity of a company's investments.

Elevator Pitch: An elevator pitch is a brief, persuasive speech that is given to potential investors in order to attract funding. This speech should be no more than a few minutes long and should highlight the company's business plan and investment potential.

Employee Stock Ownership Program (ESOP): An ESOP is a company-sponsored plan that allows employees to own shares in the company - which can include options, Restricted Stock Units (RSUs) or other instruments. This plan allows employees to participate in the company's success and helps to create a sense of ownership in the company. ESOPs are often used as a way to reward employees and promote loyalty.* When people talk about 'startup equity', they are often talking about options; *see Week 6, Day 4 and Week 8, Day 3 along with the link document since this is a frequent concept* [See 'Options']

Exercise Price (Strike Price): An exercise price, also known as a strike price, is the price at which a stock option can be exercised. This is the price that must be paid in order to purchase the shares underlying the option. The exercise price is set when the option is first created and can be increased or decreased over time.

Exit Event (Liquidity Event): An exit event, also known as a liquidity event, is the point at which a company is able to sell its assets or go public. This event allows a company to receive cash in order to pay off its debts and distribute profits to its shareholders. An exit event can be triggered by a number of factors, such as a sale of the company or an initial public offering (IPO).*

Fair Market Value: A fair market value is the price at which a security can be exchanged between two parties, both of whom are acting rationally and know all the relevant information about the security. In venture capital, this price is usually based on the previous round of funding. If a company has not had a previous funding round, sometimes investors need to perform a 409a valuation to assign a fair market value.*

Fiduciary: A fiduciary is a person who is responsible for managing the money and property of another person. In venture capital, fiduciaries are responsible for protecting the interests of their investors. This includes making sure that the company is being run efficiently and that its investments are being managed properly. Fiduciaries are also responsible for ensuring that the company is complying with all applicable laws and regulations.

First Refusal Rights: First refusal rights are a contractual provision that gives investors the right to sell their shares back to the company at a predetermined price. This provision allows investors to sell their shares back to the company in order to protect their investment in case of a down round.

Friends and Family Round: A friends and family round is a type of financing round in which the company solicits investments from its friends and family members. This round is typically used to raise a small amount of money and is often used as a way to test the waters before seeking outside funding.*

Full Ratchet: A full ratchet is a contractual provision that allows investors to increase their ownership in the company if the company issues new shares at a lower price than the original investment. This provision ensures that investors maintain their proportional ownership in the company no matter how the company's stock performs.

Fully Diluted: Fully diluted in venture capital means that all outstanding options and warrants have been exercised, and all convertible debt has been converted into equity.

Fund of Funds: A fund of funds is a type of investment fund that invests in other investment funds. This type of fund allows investors to gain access to a variety of investment opportunities without having to invest in each individual fund. Fund of funds are often used as a way to reduce risk and exposure to individual investments.

Grandfather Rights: Grandfather rights are a contractual provision that gives investors the right to maintain their ownership in the company if new investors are brought in at a lower price. This provision ensures that investors do not lose their proportional ownership in the company no matter how the company's stock performs.

GP (General Partner): A general partner in venture capital is a person that leads up and invests on behalf of a venture capital fund.

They are responsible for finding new investment opportunities and monitoring the performance of the companies in which the fund has invested. GPs are typically paid a management fee and a percentage of the profits generated by the fund.*

General Solicitation: General solicitation within venture capital is the act of publicly advertising an investment opportunity to a wide audience. This type of solicitation is often used to attract new investors and can be done through a variety of methods, such as online advertising, print media, or even word-of-mouth. Complying with general solicitation laws are important for most institutional investors.*

Gross Margin: Gross margin is a financial metric that measures the profitability of a company's products and services. It is calculated by subtracting the cost of goods sold from the total revenue and dividing the result by the total revenue. Gross margin can be used to assess a company's overall profitability and to compare the profitability of different products and services.*

Growth Equity: Growth equity is a type of investment in which the investor focuses on the growth potential of the company rather than its profitability. This type of investment is often used to help companies expand their operations and grow their business. Growth equity investors invest in companies that are farther along in the lifecycle compared to traditional venture capital funds.

K-1: A Schedule K-1 (often referred to simply as a "K-1") is a tax document that helps investors in venture funds calculate their tax obligation for the year. Venture funds are responsible for sending K-1s to all of their investors every year.

Key Man Clause: A key man clause is a contractual provision that allows investors to exit their investment if the company loses its key employee. This provision protects investors in the event that the company's most important employee leaves, and helps ensure that they do not lose any money as a result of the departure.

Incubator: A startup incubator is a business or organization that provides mentorship and support to early-stage startups. Incubators typically offer office space, mentorship, and access to funding and resources.*

Information Rights: Information rights are the rights of investors to receive regular updates on the progress of the company and its investments. This type of information helps investors stay informed about the health of their investment and makes it easier to track their return on investment.

Initial Public Offering (IPO): An initial public offering (IPO) is the process by which a company sells its shares to the public for the first time. IPOs are often used to raise money for the company and to increase its visibility and credibility. This is what 'listing' often means, and is a sign of a successful exit for early-stage investors.

Inside Round: An inside round is a type of investment in which the investor is already invested and is familiar with the company and its management team. This type of investment is often used to help companies expand their operations and grow their business, and due to the information advantage, are usually done through shorter processes.

Investment Syndicate: An investment syndicate is a group of investors that team up to invest in a company. This type of investment is often used to help companies expand their operations and grow their business. Syndicates are typically less risky for investors and provide a higher return on investment.

JOBS Act: The JOBS act is a piece of legislation that was passed in 2012 with the goal of making it easier for startups to raise money. The act made it legal for startups to solicit investments from the general public, and it also simplified the process for registering with the SEC.*

Letter of Intent (LOI): A letter of intent is a document that outlines the terms of an agreement between two or more parties. It is typically used to negotiate and finalize a deal (often an acquisition), and can be used to outline everything from the financial details to the specific provisions of the agreement.*

Limited Partner (LP): A limited partner is an investor in a venture fund who does not have any management rights or influence in the company. This type of investor typically has a smaller stake in the company and a lower risk profile.*

Lead Investor: A lead investor is an investor who has a significant stake in the company and a high risk profile. This type of investor typically provides the majority of the capital for the round and has a large influence on the company's operations.*

Liquidation: Liquidation is the process of selling off all of a company's assets. This process typically occurs either when a company has a positive liquidation event (IPO or M&A) or when a company becomes insolvent and can no longer afford to operate.

Liquidation Preference: Liquidation preference is a term used in venture capital to describe the order in which investors are repaid their investment in the event of a liquidation. Typically, investors will have a liquidation preference that gives them first priority when it comes to receiving their money back. This is a protective measure used by investors to ensure they do not lose money as a result of the liquidation.

Lock-Up Period: A lock-up period is a time period during which company insiders are not allowed to sell their shares. This is a measure used by companies to prevent insiders from cashing out their shares immediately after the company goes public.*

LPA: A limited partner agreement is a contract between a limited partner and a venture capital firm. The agreement outlines the financial details of the investment and specifies the rights and responsibilities of both parties.

Management Fee: A management fee is a fee that is paid to the company's management team for their services. This fee is typically a percentage of the assets under management, and this fee is paid annually across the lifetime of the fund. The standard management fee is 2% per year.*

Memorandum of Understanding (MOU): A memorandum of understanding is a document that outlines the terms of an agreement between two or more parties. It is typically used to negotiate and finalize a deal, and can be used to outline everything from the financial details to the specific provisions of the agreement.

MRR (Monthly Recurring Revenue): This measures the amount of monthly revenue that is coming in through subscriptionsMRR is arguably the most important metric for software-as-a-service companies.*

'No Shop' Clause: A no-shop clause is a term used in venture capital to describe a provision in an agreement that prohibits the company from seeking offers from other investors. This clause is designed to protect the interests of the lead investor and ensures that they are the only party with which the company can negotiate.

Net Revenue: Net revenue is the total amount of revenue that a company generates after deducting all of the costs associated with generating that revenue. This figure represents the amount of money that a company has available to pay its expenses and reinvest in its business.

Non-Disclosure Agreement (NDA): A non-disclosure agreement is a legal contract between two or more parties that prohibits them from sharing any confidential information about the deal or the parties involved. This agreement is typically used in negotiations to protect the interests of the parties involved.

OA (Operating Agreement): An operating agreement is a contract between the limited partners and the venture capital firm that outlines the financial details of the investment. It also specifies the rights and responsibilities of both parties.

Option Pool: An option pool is a set of shares that are set aside for the purpose of granting options to employees and advisors. This pool is typically created when a company is founded, and the shares are then granted to employees and advisors as options over a period of time. [Related to ESOP]*

Over-Allotment Option: An over-allotment option is an option that the lead investor has the right to purchase additional shares from the company in the event that there is excess demand from investors. This option gives the lead investor the opportunity to increase their ownership in the company and ensures that they maintain a controlling stake.

Pari Passu: Pari passu is a term used in venture capital to describe a provision in a term sheet that requires investors to participate in subsequent financing rounds on a pro-rata basis.*

Participating Preferred Stock: Participating preferred stock is a type of preferred stock that gives the holders the right to receive dividends and to participate in the company's profits. This type of stock typically has a higher dividend rate than regular preferred stock, and the holders have first priority when it comes to receiving their money back in the event of a liquidation.

Party Round: Party round occur in early financing rounds when companies raise large amounts of money from a large number of different investors instead of raising from a smaller group of investors.

Pay to Play: Pay to play is a term used in venture capital to describe a provision in a term sheet that requires investors to participate in subsequent financing rounds on a pro-rata basis.

Piggyback Registration Rights: Piggyback registration rights are a type of registration right that allows investors to register their shares with the SEC on the same Form S-3 used by the company. This option is typically granted to investors who participate in a company's Series A round of financing.

Portfolio Company: A portfolio company is a company that has received money from investors in order to grow and expand its business. Venture capitalists invest in these companies with the hope of achieving a return on their investment through an eventual exit event, such as an initial public offering (IPO) or a sale of the company.

Post-Money Valuation: Post-money valuation is the value of a company after it has raised money from investors. This figure includes the amount of money that has been raised, as well as the value of the company's existing equity.* *See Week 6 Day 2 and Day 4*

Preemptive Rights: Preemptive rights are a type of right that allows investors to maintain their ownership percentage in a company by purchasing shares in subsequent rounds of financing on a pro-rata basis. This option ensures that the investors have an opportunity to maintain their ownership stake in the company and prevents them from losing out on future opportunities.*

Preferred Stock: Preferred stock is a type of stock that gives the holders certain rights, such as the right to receive dividends and to participate in the company's profits. This type of stock typically has a higher dividend rate than regular stock, and the holders have first priority when it comes to receiving their money back in the event of a liquidation.

Pre-Money Valuation: Pre-money valuation is the value of a company before it has raised money from investors. This figure includes the amount of money that is being raised, as well as the value of the company's existing equity.*

Pre-Seed Funding: Pre-seed funding is typically the first round of financing for startups. This often comes from angel investors, accelerators, incubators, startup studios, or early-stage VCs.*

Price Anti-Dilution Protection: Price anti-dilution protection is a term used in venture capital to describe a provision in a term sheet that protects investors from having their ownership percentage diluted in future rounds of financing. This provision ensures that the investors maintain their ownership stake in the company and prevents them from losing out on future opportunities. *See Week 6 chapters*

Protective Provisions: Protective provisions are a set of clauses in a term sheet that protect the interests of the investors. These provisions ensure that the investors maintain their ownership stake in the company and prevent them from losing out on future opportunities.

Private Placement: A private placement is a type of investment that is made by a large number of investors in a company that is not open to the general public. This type of investment is typically made through a private placement memorandum, which is a document that contains information about the company and the terms of the investment.

Pro-Rata Rights: Pro-rata rights are a type of right that allows investors to maintain their ownership percentage in a company by purchasing shares in subsequent rounds of financing on a pro-rata basis. This option ensures that the investors have an opportunity to maintain their ownership stake in the company and prevents them from losing out on future opportunities.*

Qualified IPO: A Qualified IPO is an initial public offering that is registered with the Securities and Exchange Commission (SEC) and meets all of the requirements specified in the JOBS Act. This type of IPO is open to all investors, regardless of their income or net worth.

Ratchet: A ratchet is a clause in a term sheet that allows the investors to maintain their ownership percentage in a company by purchasing shares in subsequent rounds of financing.

Redemption Rights (Redeemable): Redemption rights describe a provision that allows the investor to sell their shares back to the company at a predetermined price. This provision gives the investors the option to cash out their investment and provides them with some protection in case the company does not perform well.*

Registration Rights: Registration rights are a type of right that allows investors to register their shares with the Securities and Exchange Commission (SEC) so that they can sell them to the general public. This provision gives the investors the ability to liquidate their investment and provides them with some protection in case the company does not perform well. It can help private investors get access to a broader range of buyers.

Repurchase Option: A repurchase option is a clause in a term sheet that gives the company the right to buy back the shares of the investors at a predetermined price. This provision gives the company the ability to regain control of its shares and prevents the investors from selling them to the general public.

Restricted Stock (RSU): A restricted stock is a type of security that is given to employees of a company as part of their compensation. This type of stock typically cannot be sold or traded for a certain period of time, and the holder is required to forfeit the stock if they leave the company.

Return on Investment (ROI): ROI is a metric that is used to measure the profitability of an investment. It is calculated by dividing the amount of money that has been made by the amount of money that has been invested.

Revenue Multiple: Revenue multiple is a metric that is used to measure the attractiveness of an investment. It is calculated by dividing the company's revenue by the amount of money that has been invested. This metric gives investors a sense of how much money they can expect to make from their investment.

Revenue Run Rate: Revenue run rate is an indicator of financial performance that takes a company's performance over a certain period (week, month, quarter) and converts it to an annual number for simple math. An example would be a company generating $10,000 in revenue over the quarter would have a $40,000 revenue run rate for the year.

Right of First Refusal (ROFR): A right of first refusal is a clause in a term sheet that gives the company the right to buy back the shares of the investors at a predetermined price. This provision gives the company the ability to regain control of its shares and prevents the investors from selling them to the general public.*

Road Show: A road show is a series of presentations that a company makes to potential investors in order to attract funding for their business. The presentations are typically made by the company's CEO or CFO and provide an overview of the business and its financials.

Rule 506(b): Rule 506(b) is a provision in the United States Code that allows companies to raise money from accredited investors without registering with the SEC. This provision provides companies with some flexibility when raising money and makes it easier for them to get funding from accredited investors.

SAFE Note: A SAFE note is a type of security that is used to raise money from investors. It is similar to a convertible note, but it has fewer restrictions and is easier to understand. *See Week 6*

Super Pro Rata: Super pro rata is a term that refers to the right of a shareholder to maintain or increase their ownership stake in the company even if the company issues new shares of stock. This term is typically used in the context of a rights offering, where the shareholders are given the opportunity to purchase new shares of stock at a discounted price.

Side Letter: A side letter is a supplemental agreement that is entered into between the company and the investors. This agreement typically contains more detailed information about the terms of the investment than what is found in the term sheet.*

Seed Round: A seed round is the initial round of funding that a company receives from investors. This round is typically used to finance the development of the company's product and to hire the initial employees.*

Senior Liquidation Preference: A senior liquidation preference is a clause in a term sheet that gives the investors seniority over the other shareholders in the event of a liquidation. This provision ensures that the investors will get their money back before any other shareholders receive anything.

Series A: Series A funding is the first major round of funding for a startup. It typically follows a seed round, in which the company raises smaller amounts of money from family, friends, and angel investors. It's succeeded by a Series B funding round, Series C, and so on.

Separation Agreement: A separation agreement is a contract that is signed by the company and the investors when they split up. This agreement outlines the terms of the separation and ensures that both parties are protected legally.

Shareholder Agreement: A shareholder agreement is a contract that is signed by the company and the shareholders when they split up. This agreement outlines the terms of the separation and ensures that both parties are protected legally.

Shareholder Limit: A shareholder limit is a provision in a term sheet that sets a limit on the number of shareholders the company can have. This provision protects the investors from having too many shareholders and diluting their ownership stake.

Shareholder of Record: A shareholder of record is a shareholder who is registered with the company's secretary and is listed on the company's share register. This person has the rights and obligations associated with being a shareholder and is typically the person who receives dividends and voting rights.

Shares Outstanding: Shares outstanding refers to the number of shares that a company has issued and are currently owned by investors. This term is typically used when discussing a liquidation event, such as a sale or an IPO, where the shareholders would receive money based on their ownership stake.

Stacked Preference: A stacked preference is a provision in a term sheet that gives the investors priority over the other shareholders in the event of a liquidation. This provision ensures that the investors will get their money back before any other shareholders receive anything.

S-3 Registration Rights: S-3 registration rights are a provision in a term sheet that gives the company the right to register their shares with the SEC. This right allows the company to sell their shares to the public and raise money from investors.

Tag-Along Rights: Tag-along rights are a provision in a term sheet that gives the shareholders the right to sell their shares to the company at the same price as the investors. This provision ensures that the shareholders will receive the same price as the investors in the event of a sale or an IPO.

Term Sheet: A term sheet is a document that is used to negotiate the terms of an investment. This document lays out the key provisions of the investment, such as the amount of money being invested, the valuation of the company, and the rights of the shareholders.

Transfer Restrictions: Transfer restrictions are a provision in a term sheet that restricts the transfer of shares to other parties. This provision protects the investors from having their shares sold to someone who is not part of the investment agreement.

Unicorn: A unicorn is a company that has reached a billion-dollar valuation or higher.

Vesting: Vesting is a process that gradually gives employees ownership of their stock options over a period of time. This process ensures that the employees are committed to the company and are not just cashing in their stock options and leaving.*

Warrant: A warrant is a type of security that gives the holder the right to purchase shares of stock at a predetermined price. This contract is typically used by investors who are looking to invest in a company.*

Warrant Coverage: Warrant coverage is a provision in a term sheet that gives investors the right to purchase more shares of stock at a predetermined price. This provision ensures that the investors will have the opportunity to increase their ownership stake in the company.*

Write-Off: A write-off happens when a portfolio company goes out of business and the fund has to mark the value of the investment as zero.*